WHY ISN'T GOD ANSWERING ME?

WHY ISN'T GOD ANSWERING ME?

GERALD N. LUND

DESERET
BOOK

Salt Lake City, Utah

Library of Congress Cataloging-in-Publication Data
Names: Lund, Gerald N., author.
Title: Why isn't God answering me? / Gerald N. Lund.
Description: Salt Lake City, Utah : Deseret Book, [2018] | Includes bibliographical references and index.
Identifiers: LCCN 2018005157 | ISBN 9781629724492 (hardbound : alk. paper)
Subjects: LCSH: Prayer—The Church of Jesus Christ of Latter-day Saints. | Spiritual life—The Church of Jesus Christ of Latter-day Saints. | The Church of Jesus Christ of Latter-day Saints—Doctrines. | Mormon Church—Doctrines.
Classification: LCC BX8656 .L86 2018 | DDC 248.4/89332—dc23
LC record available at https://lccn.loc.gov/2018005157

Printed in the United States of America
Publishers Printing, Salt Lake City, UT

10   9   8   7   6   5   4   3   2   1

CONTENTS

PART III
MEETING THE CONDITIONS SET BY THE LORD

PART IV
DRAWING ON THE POWERS OF HEAVEN

OUR QUEST

Most readers of this book will have what we shall call "believing hearts." If you purchased this book, or had it given or loaned to you, you are most likely a person who believes (or at least wants to believe) in a loving God who watches over and blesses His children. That belief profoundly affects how you live your life. You want to be good so that your life is pleasing to Him. You seek to exercise faith in Him and believe that when you do that, you are a happier person and will be blessed for doing so.

However, there may be some readers who are not so sure about God and how they relate to Him right now. Some may wonder if He exists at all. Others believe He does, but they're not sure what kind of God He really is. Some ask why, if there is a God, there is so much suffering in the world. Others may have trusted Him in times past, but when life took one of those hard turns, which it so often does, they cried unto Him, pled with Him to help, even begged Him to intervene, and nothing happened. And so they turned away, their hearts filled with frustration, anger, and doubt.

This book is for any and all who either are now asking or have sometime in the past asked this almost universal question. Janice Kapp Perry, in a wonderful song written for Primary children, captured this deep longing we have in words that speak to all of us: "Heavenly Father, are you really there? And do you hear and answer every child's prayer?"

Even those with great faith are not immune from these questions. Here are the cries of the Prophet Joseph Smith and of the Redeemer Himself:

"O God, where art thou?" (D&C 121:1).

"My God, my God, why hast thou forsaken me?" (Matthew 27:46).

We believe it is a question that can be answered in many ways. And that is the primary purpose of this book—to answer this very simple but heart-wrenching cry for understanding:

WHY ISN'T GOD ANSWERING ME?

ABOUT THIS BOOK

1. *This book is narrowly limited in its scope.* It is not intended to be a treatise on personal revelation but rather a focus on one particular aspect of revelation: getting answers to our prayers.

2. *This book will largely ignore the more obvious reasons why God isn't answering our prayers.* It will quickly become apparent that we don't discuss much about the more serious forms of sin and wickedness in this book. We only briefly mention such things as moral cleanliness, marital infidelity, criminal behavior of all kinds, pornography, family neglect, other forms of abuse, and so on. We do this because experience shows that those who are participating in these more serious sins either are not concerned about God and what He thinks of them, do not consider their behavior to be bad, or already know that these more serious sins are why God isn't

currently answering their prayers. Our focus, therefore, will be on those things that are not so obvious, things that we may acknowledge as bad habits or human frailties and weaknesses but that we do not necessarily consider to be sinful behavior in the traditional sense. Therefore, we may not even consider them as things that are causing this blockage in getting answers to our prayers.

3. *This book is not a call to repentance.* The reader may often *feel* that he or she is being called to repent. That is to be expected. As we talk about some of these less obvious reasons why God doesn't seem to be responding to our prayers, hopefully we will find ourselves wincing inwardly, thinking, *Oh dear. That's me. I am guilty of that one.* And when that happens, we don't need someone to tell us to change. Because of our commitment to God, we will naturally try to eliminate those things that block our access to God or more diligently facilitate those things that increase the likelihood of getting answers to our prayers. And that desire to change is called repentance. Think of this book as a pantry of possible answers. When we are feeling a hunger for greater communion with the Spirit, this book can be a pantry where we can find something that will help us satisfy our hunger. Sometimes we find one thing that satisfies us, but on our next visit it may be something else we are looking for. Other times it may take a combination of ingredients. In other words, the purpose of the book is to help us undertake a personal assessment of where we are in our communion with God. If we do that successfully, most readers will call themselves to repentance.

4. *This book will not talk a lot about how to fix whatever it is that is causing the blockage of revelation.* This may seem like a major oversight, but it will quickly become clear that this is rarely necessary, because once we identify the cause of the blockage, the solution is pretty clear. We either stop doing what is causing the

problem or start doing something that will draw us closer to God. It is as simple as that.

5. *This book does not provide all possible answers to our question.* We will discuss many possible answers to our question, but the complexity of human nature is such that the number of possible answers could run into the hundreds. We could not possibly describe every reason why people aren't getting answers to their prayers. But we will try to deal with some of the more common reasons that may be the source of our problem. Asking the Lord, "Where do I start?" or, "What next?" is always a good idea, because He does have *all* the answers.

6. *On the surface, some of the answers may seem more trivial than others.* Don't be surprised if from time to time you find yourself saying, "Really? Something that simple could be what's holding me back?" Lehi and his family said something similar when they discovered the Liahona outside Lehi's tent. Nephi, however, saw it for what it was when he said, "And thus we see that by *small means* the Lord can bring about great things" (1 Nephi 16:29; emphasis added).

7. *This book does not need to be read from start to finish.* Some readers may choose to browse through the book rather than read it sequentially. Others may start with the table of contents and then go to a chapter that particularly catches their interest. Remember our pantry analogy. Feel free to enter, to look around, and to choose what best satisfies your hunger.

8. *The ultimate purpose of this book is to encourage all of us to constantly ask two questions of the Lord.* If we remember to always ask two specific questions, miracles can happen: "What can I *start* doing that will increase my ability to receive answers to my prayers?" and, "What do I need to *stop* doing because it is hampering my ability to receive answers to my prayers?"

As a final note, throughout the book, many quotations have portions that are emphasized through the use of italics. When the emphasis is in the original source, that will be noted. All other times, the emphasis is added by the author.

I

WHY? WHY? WHY?

CHAPTER 1

"O GOD, WHERE ART THOU?"

———— ✑ ————

*"If [we] are acquainted with the revelations, there
is no question—personal or social or political or
occupational—that need go unanswered. Therein is
contained the fulness of the everlasting gospel. Therein
we find principles of truth that resolve every confusion
and every problem and every dilemma that will face
the human family or any individual in it."*

—BOYD K. PACKER[1]

THE MIND AND WILL OF GOD

Joseph Smith once made two simple declarations about revelation: "We never can comprehend the things of God and of heaven, but by revelation"[2] and, "Salvation cannot come without revelation; it is in vain for anyone to minister without it."[3] Elder Bruce R. McConkie summarized it this way: "God is known only by revelation. God stands revealed or he remains forever unknown."[4]

It takes only a moment of reflection to realize that without the principle of revelation there would be no Church of Jesus Christ of Latter-day Saints, no Sacred Grove, no angel Moroni, no modern scripture, no temples, no ordinances. Nothing.

Revelation is defined as the process by which God shares His mind and will with His children through the medium of the Holy Ghost. Since God, by nature, wants only those things that will bring us ultimate joy, revelation is how He guides and directs us to that end.

The significance of revelation also has profound implications for each one of us as individuals. Just as the Church would not exist without revelation, no individual can find ultimate happiness and joy without receiving inspiration and

"I am convinced that there is no simple formula or technique that I could give you that would immediately facilitate your mastering the ability to be guided by the Holy Spirit. Our Father expects you to learn how to obtain that divine help by exercising faith in Him and His Holy Son. . . . He knows that essential personal growth will come as you struggle to learn how to be led by the Spirit. That struggle will develop your immortal character as you perfect your capacity to identify His will in your life through the whisperings of the Holy Ghost."

—RICHARD G. SCOTT[5]

revelation from on high. It is revelation from God that enlivens the Church and our individual lives.

Four Fundamental Truths about Personal Revelation

Before we turn our attention to the question that serves as the title of this book, let us quickly review four principles that govern the flow of personal revelation. We shall seek to apply these general principles to our specific question, which is how to increase our ability to get answers to our prayers.

1. *There are three aspects of the process of revelation.* We could call these the three R's of revelation. First, we must *receive* revelation. Second, we must *recognize* revelation for what it is when it does come. Third, we must *respond* to that revelation if we expect to receive more. All three of these are true of prayer as well. We need to be in a position where God will send us revelation. But we also need to learn how to recognize answers to our prayers when they come in unexpected ways. And, finally, if we ignore direction from the Lord when He gives it to us, our lack of response may be the answer to our question, "Why isn't God answering me?"

2. *God determines all aspects of revelation.* As noted, by definition, revelation is the sharing of God's mind and will with us. This means that revelation is always unidirectional: it flows *from* God *to* us, never in the reverse direction. Since God has perfect knowledge, we can never reveal anything to Him. We can't kneel at our bedside and pour out our hearts to God about our problem and have Him say, "Oh! I didn't know that." So, God decides to *whom* revelation is given, *when* it is given, in what *form* it is given, and what *content* is shared.

Jacob taught: "Seek not to counsel the Lord, but to take counsel from his hand" (Jacob 4:10). Often, this may be the reason that we're got getting answers. We try to tell God how, or when, or in what form we want our answer to come. Sorry, but that is not our privilege.

3. *The voice of the Lord is unique and not always easily recognizable.* It is possible that we simply don't recognize answers to our prayers when God gives them to us. We shall discuss this concept in Chapter 4.

4. *There is counterfeit revelation.* This principle and how it affects getting answers to our prayers will be more fully explored in Chapter 3.

PRAYER AND REVELATION

A fifth principle of revelation is that God specifically invites us to communicate with Him through the medium of prayer. In the scriptures, one of the most oft-repeated commandments is that we are to pray to Him. Jesus said: "Ask, and it shall be given you; seek, and ye shall find; knock, and it shall be opened unto you" (Matthew 7:7). Note that all three of those phrases contain a commandment *and* a specific promise: *Ask* and it shall be given. *Seek* and we shall find. *Knock* and it shall be opened. That admonition and others like it are found literally hundreds of times throughout the scriptures and in the words of modern prophets. We pray to Him; He answers us through the Holy Spirit. If we get frustrated because God doesn't seem to be answering us, sometimes we decide that we will stop praying. That is like a child saying, "School is too hard. I thought I would learn things. I'm not going to school anymore."

When we think about it, we realize prayer is an astonishing privilege. God is the Supreme Being in the universe. He is the Creator of all things and upholds all things by a perfect and infinite combination of power, knowledge, love, and justice. He is a Being of glorious, infinite majesty. And yet He invites us, very finite, self-centered, weak, sinful, and foolish creatures, to approach Him directly in prayer. Unlike the way things work in the world, we don't have to wait until we are a certain age. God doesn't hold certain "office hours." He is never gone on vacation. We don't have to go through an automated phone system that gives us various options to choose from before reaching someone who can help us. It doesn't matter which language we speak; He understands them all. He can even read our thoughts when we don't pray aloud.

Why does He offer us that privilege? The answer is really quite simple. It is because He is our Father. Some in the world believe that concept is only metaphorical. That is, they think that God is *like* a caring, loving father. We believe that we are His *literal* offspring. This is why Jesus told us to address God as "*Our Father* which art in heaven" (Matthew 6:9).

A Dilemma and a Challenge for the Faithful

The invitation for us to pray to our Heavenly Father directly whenever we wish, concerning any problem we have, and to expect that He will actually hear us and respond to us, is really quite astonishing. And it would be well for us, as we thank Him for the many blessings we receive from His hand, to also thank Him for this gift of direct communion with Him.

But with prayer, there frequently comes a challenge and a dilemma. It is simply this: We accept His invitation to pray to Him and do so regularly and earnestly. But sometimes, when we are praying for a particular blessing or asking for help in solving a particularly vexing problem, nothing seems to happen. If we persist in this quest and still nothing comes, we begin to ask, "Am I just not

"We need strength beyond ourselves to keep the commandments in whatever circumstance life brings to us. The combination of trials and their duration are as varied as are the children of our Heavenly Father. No two are alike. But what is being tested is the same, at all times in our lives and for every person: will we do whatsoever the Lord our God will command us?"

—HENRY B. EYRING[6]

hearing Him?" Or, "Have I done something to offend Him?" Or, "Is it because I am not in tune and just can't hear His answer?" Or, "*Why* isn't God answering me?"

This is especially troubling if we come to Him laden with the burdens of life. We plead for direction on major decisions or relief from pain and suffering, and it feels as if the heavens are made of brass. As adversity and tribulation engulf us, we plead with Him to come to our aid, but nothing changes. We seek solace in times of great sorrow, to no avail.

Ironically, as noted in the preface, this dilemma is unique to people of faith. Those who don't believe in God, or who doubt that He troubles Himself with the problems of mere humans, typically do not ask such questions. In fact, they often scoff at those of us who do pray, saying, "He is not answering *because He is not there or He doesn't care!*"

But to the believer, it is not that simple. These questions can create a crisis of faith. Here are actual accounts from believing people who have found themselves in this dilemma:

A sixteen-year-old girl. "When I was fifteen, my father was diagnosed with terminal cancer. I have never prayed so hard about anything in my life. He received several priesthood blessings and we had ward, stake, and family fasts for him. After suffering months and months of terrible pain, he passed away. After that, I decided that maybe there is no God, or at least not one who hears and answers our prayers. So I stopped attending church and I stopped praying."

A mother of five children. "When my husband and I started getting serious in our courtship, I received what I felt was a strong confirmation that he was the one I should marry. We were married in the temple. Recently my husband announced that he is gay and is leaving the Church. He wants a divorce so he can marry and live with his new partner. If God knew this would eventually happen, why didn't He warn me not to marry him?"

A young man in his early twenties. "I was dating this wonderful girl that I loved deeply. She was everything that I wanted—a wonderful woman, strong in the faith, someone who would make a great mother. For months I prayed to know if she was the right one for me. I never got a clear answer, so I decided the answer must be no, and I broke it off with her. Did I do the right thing or was I just plain stupid?"

Parents in their late fifties. "Many years ago, our daughter, then in her early twenties, turned away from God. Soon she was into all kinds of self-destructive behavior. We have prayed for her every day since, but nothing changes. It has been two years since we last heard from her. We don't even know if she is still alive. It feels as though God has not only abandoned her, but us too."

A married couple in their mid-thirties. "Before we were married, my wife and I decided that we would take as many children as the Lord chose to send us. But as the years went on, no children came. We tried everything. We fasted and prayed more times than we can count. Our testimonies are still strong, but we can't help but ask: Some women are aborting their children. Children are being sent into homes where they will be abused, neglected, or starved. Couldn't God send even one of these children to our home?"

A young business executive in his early forties. "I came up with a great idea for a new software program and went to work developing it. After much prayer and fasting, we decided to create a startup company. We launched in the fall of 2006. Things went well for a while, and we were raking in the money. Then the global financial crisis of 2007–2008 hit. We lost everything. The hardest thing I've ever done in my life was try to explain to my sixteen-year-old son why we were moving in with Grandma."

A single LDS woman, graduate degrees, professional career. "I grew up in a large family, all of whom are still faithful in the kingdom. All of my brothers and sisters have married in the temple and have numerous children. I am turning forty this year. I am resigned to the fact that I will likely never marry in this life. I understand and believe that I will find a righteous husband in the next life, but that is only partially comforting. Even after all these years, I sometimes ask, 'Why me, Lord? Was I not faithful enough?'"

The above challenges are diverse, but the questions that naturally come from such circumstances are heart-wrenching and filled with anguish. In this book we shall explore possible reasons we are not getting answers to our prayers.

CHAPTER 2

BE NOT CAST DOWN

───※───

"Look up, my soul; be not cast down.
Keep not thine eyes upon the ground.
Break off the shackles of the earth.
Receive, my soul, the spirit's birth."

—"Before Thee, Lord, I Bow My Head"[7]

EXCESSIVE GUILT, UNJUSTIFIED SHAME, AND UNWARRANTED DISCOURAGEMENT

Before we begin our quest to understand why God may not be answering our prayers even when we are striving to be faithful, there is something that needs to be noted.

The standards set in the gospel are very demanding. In one place we are told that we are to be perfect, even as Jesus and His Father are perfect (see Matthew 5:48; 3 Nephi 12:48). Fortunately, our prophets have made it clear that while this is an ultimate goal, it is not something we fully achieve in this life. Joseph F. Smith once said: "We do not look for absolute perfection in man. Mortal man is not capable of being absolutely perfect."[8]

Nevertheless, there is a natural tendency for us to see ourselves forever falling short of God's expectations, even when we are not. We acknowledge that God "cannot look upon sin with the least degree of allowance" (D&C 1:31), but we also need to remember that God is "merciful and gracious, longsuffering, and abundant in goodness and truth" (Exodus 34:6). In another place we are told that God is "slow to anger" (Psalm 103:8).

In the *Lectures on Faith,* Joseph Smith made a significant observation about the importance of understanding these attributes: "Those who know their weakness and liability to sin would be in constant doubt of salvation if it were not for the idea which they have of the excellency of the character of God, that he is *slow to anger* and *long-suffering,* and of a *forgiving disposition,* and does forgive iniquity, transgression, and sin. An idea of these facts does away doubt, and makes faith exceedingly strong."[9]

Since none of us is perfect, there is always something in our lives that is out of harmony with God's will. If we don't balance that realization with faith in God's mercy and His long-suffering nature, we can be stricken with *excessive* guilt, *unjustified* shame, and *unwarranted* discouragement. These emotions can dampen our ability to receive revelation and/or get answers to our prayers. And Satan, knowing that, is always there to goad us into feeling that we are failing because we are not perfect.

It is a natural tendency in some people to view themselves more negatively than God views them. Therefore they feel more guilt, shame, discouragement, and sometimes even hopelessness than is justified by their actions.

When a young man who was immersed in pornography was asked by his bishop to earnestly pray for God's help in overcoming his addiction, the young man said that he was not worthy to approach God in prayer. Those feelings were certainly not coming from our Father in Heaven.

Back when the Relief Society had what they called "spiritual living" lessons, one woman came home and said to her husband, "I have this curious ambivalence about the spiritual living lessons. I always feel so good when I listen to them, but I always come home so depressed about myself, because I see so many things that I'm not doing right."

As an adult fireside was about to begin, with a wry smile, a woman told the speaker, who was a good friend, "John, if you

"As children of God, we should not demean or vilify ourselves, as if beating up on ourselves is somehow going to make us the person God wants us to become. No! With a willingness to repent and a desire for increased righteousness always in our hearts, I would hope we could pursue personal improvement in a way that doesn't include getting ulcers or anorexia, feeling depressed or demolishing our self-esteem. That is not what the Lord wants for Primary children or anyone else who honestly sings, 'I'm trying to be like Jesus.'"

—JEFFREY R. HOLLAND[10]

tell me one more thing I need to do right now to be a faithful Latter-day Saint, I may stand up in the middle of your lecture and scream."

Don't we all feel that way sometimes? And that is a good thing, in a way. One of the functions of the Holy Ghost is to sensitize us to the difference between good and evil. It is the righteous person who feels his or her sins most keenly. As C. S. Lewis put it: "The right direction [in a person's life] leads not only to peace but to knowledge. When a man is getting better he understands more and more clearly the evil that is still left in him. When a man is getting worse, he understands his own badness less and less."[11]

One father described how he learned this principle for himself: "Feeling that our family home evenings were not going very well, I decided that one of the reasons was because I was failing in my role as head of the home because I was too busy to pay the price to prepare. Too often it was a hectic, slapped together, 'what-can-we-do-tonight?' experience. So one Monday I really made an effort to change that pattern. I carefully prepared what I thought would be a great lesson for my young family. I had visual aids and ways for the children to participate.

"As it turned out, the opening prayer was the highlight of the night. Things unraveled so quickly that I ended up yelling at the children and sending them all to their rooms before five minutes had passed. I laugh about that now, but I wasn't laughing that night. As we prepared for bed later, I said to my wife, 'What's the use? I try and try and yet I'm a failure as a father.' She noted that she felt the same discouragement.

"Just a week later, I was in Northern California on an assignment for my occupation. Early one morning I was at the San Francisco International Airport waiting for my return flight to Los Angeles. As I sat there, my thoughts returned to that disastrous family home evening and feelings of guilt and shame and discouragement washed over me again. In the midst of those feelings, my attention was drawn to a group of people coming down the concourse toward the gate area (this was long before security stopped letting non-passengers go into the terminal).

"I was surprised to see a group of four or five young people who looked to be in their mid-teens. They were loud, noisy, and brash and were accosting people for money. They carried signs that said they were living on the streets and that they hadn't eaten for two days or more. They were a pretty motley-looking group—tattered, soiled clothing; lots of tattoos; rings in their noses, lips, eyebrows, ears, and navels.

"As they moved closer, a policeman appeared down the concourse and yelled something at them. They quickly melted away. As I watched them leave, two thoughts came to my mind in quick succession. First, earlier that week, I had read an article in the newspaper called 'Throwaway Kids.' The article described thousands of youth in the San Francisco area who lived on the streets. These had not *run* away from home. Their parents had *thrown* them out of the house and told them never to come back. And here they were, just a few feet away from me. It was a shocking confirmation of a shocking reality.

"As things settled down again, another thought came to me. It hit me hard as well. It was this: *And you think you are failing as a father because you had a disastrous family home evening last week?*

"It was a powerful, revelatory moment," he concluded. "Yes, there were things in my life that I could be and should be doing better. Yes, we needed to try harder to have meaningful family home evenings and have family prayer and scripture reading more consistently." But, as the father could now see, things weren't really as bad as he had thought.

None of us is perfect, but that does not mean that we are failing. Nor does it mean that God is displeased with us. And telling ourselves we are failing is Satan's mantra, not Heavenly Father's.

Let us strive to strike an important balance between knowing our failings so we can improve ourselves and condemning ourselves more harshly that God Himself does. Remember the words of the hymn cited above: "Look up, my soul; be not cast down."

MORE ON FEELING UNWARRANTED GUILT, SHAME, OR DISCOURAGEMENT

There is another more deeply rooted reason we may feel that God is not answering us. It is this: some individuals feel that God has forgotten them or abandoned them because they are struggling with *physiological, psychological, or emotional factors* that powerfully impact their lives. Terms such as clinical depression, severe anxiety, bipolar disorder, mental illness, and post-traumatic stress disorder describe some of these conditions. The causes of such conditions can include severe trauma, such as rape, child abuse, or combat in war; chemical imbalances in the brain; prolonged physical illness; pregnancy and childbirth; prolonged adversity; our inherited DNA; and many other causes not yet identified.

These debilitating disorders can directly impact our ability to hear the voice of the Spirit and receive answers to our prayers. Ann F. Pritt, a licensed family therapist, wrote an article for the *Ensign* titled "Healing the Spiritual Wounds of Sexual Abuse." She describes a patient of hers she calls Julia: "Having suffered from sexual abuse as a child, [Julia] struggled to reconcile her experiences with what she had been taught about Heavenly Father. She could not understand why He, being all-powerful, didn't stop the abuse. She wondered why it was so difficult for her to feel Heavenly Father's love and to recognize His answers to her prayers."

Pritt went on to say that with the help of the bishop and professional counseling, Julia is working through her painful past and is more and more able to feel Heavenly Father's love. Pritt then made this powerful observation that is relevant to our current discussion: "Many who have been abused have experiences like Julia's and find it *difficult to feel the influence of the Holy Ghost as well as to feel answers to prayer.* Although they may interpret this as a lack of Heavenly Father's love, there is another explanation. *A basic defense children use against sexual abuse is to shut down their feelings, helping them to get through the trauma. Yet this response also cuts them off from positive feelings. As a result, those who have been sexually abused may have difficulty feeling the love of Heavenly Father, His servants, and other nurturing people in their lives.*"[12]

For those of us who are close to such people, perhaps even serving as their caregivers, let us not become part of the problem by assuming their problems are of their own making or by suggesting that they just need to have more faith or try harder. Some may need prolonged professional help and prescribed medication to work through these very difficult challenges. They may also need the counsel and help of loving, patient, and understanding experts, family members, friends, and priesthood and auxiliary leaders.

To those who are suffering from physiological and psychological disorders, we suggest one other thing: focus on the healing and redemptive powers found in the Atonement of Jesus Christ. He is the One who said that His Father had sent Him "to heal the *brokenhearted,* to preach deliverance to the *captives,* . . . [and] to set at liberty them that are *bruised*" (Luke 4:18).

This is the Person who took upon Himself not only the sins of the world but also our sicknesses, afflictions, and other infirmities (see Alma 7:11–12; D&C 18:11; 2 Nephi 9:21).

Sister Pritt described another of her patients who found peace in just that way: "Carrie felt alone and misunderstood, isolated in the shame, humiliation, and pain of the abuse she had experienced. In one illuminating moment, she read that the agony of the Atonement caused the Savior, 'even God, the greatest of all, to tremble because of pain, and to bleed at every pore, and to suffer both body and spirit' (D&C 19:1). Carrie realized that she was not alone in her suffering and that the Lord had suffered far more. And she realized that He had been sent 'to heal the brokenhearted' (Luke 4:18) and that through His Atonement He could heal her wounded soul."[13]

"How many of us struggle, from time to time, with negative thoughts or feelings about ourselves? I do. It's an easy trap. Satan is the father of all lies, especially when it comes to misrepresentations about our own divine nature and purpose. Thinking small about ourselves does not serve us well. Instead it holds us back. As we've often been taught, 'No one can make you feel inferior without your consent.' We can stop comparing our worst to someone else's best. 'Comparison is the thief of joy.'"

—Joy D. Jones[14]

SUMMARY

Sister Carole M. Stephens, former First Counselor in the Relief Society General Presidency, spoke in a recent general conference on how the Master can comfort and strengthen us when we suffer from the unrighteous actions of others: "I have had many conversations with women weighed down under heavy burdens. Their covenant path from the temple has become a difficult journey of healing. They suffer from broken covenants, broken hearts, and lost confidence. Many are victims of adultery and verbal, sexual, and emotional abuse, often as the result of other people's addictions. These experiences, though no fault of their own, have left many feeling guilty and ashamed. Not understanding how to manage the powerful emotions they experience, many try to bury them, pushing them deeper into themselves. Hope and healing are not found in the dark abyss of secrecy but in the light and love of our Savior, Jesus Christ."[15]

As we begin our study of how God works with us as we pray to Him, let us keep in mind this counsel from President Russell M. Nelson: "I recognize that, on occasion, some of our most fervent prayers may seem to go unanswered. We wonder, 'Why?' I know that feeling! I know the fears and tears of such moments. But I also know that our prayers are never ignored. Our faith is never unappreciated. I know that an all-wise Heavenly Father's perspective is much broader than is ours. While we know of our mortal problems and pain, He knows of our immortal progress and potential. If we pray to know His will and submit ourselves to it with patience and courage, heavenly healing can take place in His own way and time."[16]

CHAPTER 3

COUNTERFEIT REVELATION

"Members of this church throughout the world must brace themselves for the never-ending contest between the forces of righteousness and the forces of evil."

—Harold B. Lee[17]

War in Heaven and on Earth

We know from the scriptures that when the Father presented His plan of happiness to His children, Lucifer offered to make the plan work by eliminating agency. When the Father chose His Firstborn Son to act as Savior instead, Lucifer rebelled and war broke out in heaven. He and a third part of the hosts of heaven were cast down to earth. Lucifer's name was changed to Satan, and he and his followers have continued the war ever since.

Knowing that mortality would be far too challenging and dangerous for us to get through on our own, God gave us three important sources of help along with the redemptive and enabling power of the Atonement of Jesus Christ. First, He gave the Light of Christ to all of His children so we can have a basic understanding of right and wrong. Second, for those who make covenants with Him, He offers the gift of the Holy Ghost. This gives us, if we are worthy, the personal companionship of a member of the Godhead. Third, God calls living prophets to speak for Him and to direct His work on the earth. It has been so from the time of Adam to the present day, when we are led by prophets, seers, and revelators.

But Satan knows that too. One of his prime strategic objectives is to disrupt the channel of communication between God and man in any way possible. President Boyd K. Packer made this analogy: "The first order issued by a commander mounting a military invasion is the jamming of the channels of communication of those he intends to conquer. . . . The purposes of the adversary [include] obstructing the delicate channels of revelation in both mind and spirit."[18]

Satan's primary purpose is to destroy the work of God, but knowing that will help us thwart his plans. Elder David A. Bednar put it this way: "Understanding the intent of our enemy is a key prerequisite to effective preparation."[19]

COUNTERFEIT REVELATION

Elder Mark E. Petersen, former member of the Quorum of the Twelve Apostles, taught us that one way Satan tries to confuse us is by actually giving us false messages that appear to be revelation from God: "Just as surely as the Lord, by His power, puts good ideas into our minds and entices us by them, so does Satan put evil ideas into our heads and entices us by them. I suppose we can call one 'good' revelation, and the other 'bad' revelation, can't we, because *Satan does give revelation to us, evil revelation,* to put us off the track, to lead us astray, and to ease us into sin. . . . *Satan is definitely a revelator.*"[20]

President Boyd K. Packer expanded on that concept further: "Be ever on guard lest you be deceived by inspiration from an unworthy source. You can be given false spiritual messages. There are counterfeit spirits just as there are counterfeit angels. Be careful lest you be deceived, for the devil may come disguised as an angel of light [see 2 Corinthians 11:14; D&C 129]. The spiritual part of us and the emotional part of us are so closely linked, it is possible to mistake an emotional impulse for something spiritual."[22]

"The devil also possesses power to imitate very closely this principle by which God conveys knowledge unto man, but his is the voice of the stranger, and the sheep will not follow, for they have learned and do know the voice of the true Shepherd."

—Joseph F. Smith[21]

Three things in President Packer's quote are worthy of note. First, he warns us to "be ever on guard" lest we be deceived. That suggests that the possibility of false revelation does not happen only occasionally. It is an ever-present possibility.

Second is his use of the word *counterfeit.* If something is counterfeit, it is an exact imitation of something of value that is created with the intent to deceive or defraud someone. Unless the counterfeit is clumsily done, only an expert can tell the difference between a counterfeit item and the real thing. President Packer suggests that counterfeit revelation may not be easily distinguished from the true. This is another reason to be "ever" on guard.

Third, and this is perhaps the most important point of all, he teaches us that there are actually two sources of counterfeit revelation: false spiritual messages that come directly from Satan and his followers, and our own emotions, which we confuse with true revelation.

> "All inspiration does not come from God. The evil one has the power to tap into those channels of revelation and send conflicting signals which can mislead and confuse us. There are promptings from evil sources which are so carefully counterfeited as to deceive even the very elect."
>
> —BOYD K. PACKER[23]

Here are only a few ways we may see false revelation or our own emotions manifested in ways that may confuse us:

1. Satan whispers to us that we are failing if we are not perfect (sometimes even as we pray).

2. People with no calling or authority take it upon themselves to correct others over whom they have no stewardship, who then wrongly assume that this is an answer to their prayers.

3. Due to our own ignorance or strong desires, we can think we are given doctrine contrary to the established order of the Church because it came after we prayed about it.

4. We ask God to help us in every little aspect of our lives, which is not pleasing to the Lord.

5. We want something so badly—even a good thing—that our desires take priority over God's will (for example, a lovesick boy

asking God if he should marry the girl of his dreams may assume that the answer is yes because "it feels so right" to him).

6. We accept wild rumors, false prophecies, astonishing stories, and purported revelations that spread like wildfire because they are sensational.

7. When we do get an answer to our prayers, we ignore it because it was not that dramatic.

Basically, any of the principles we discuss in this book can be counterfeited to some degree by Satan or his followers.

SUMMARY

Counterfeit revelation is one of the four fundamental complications to getting answers to our prayers. We need to remember that disrupting the channels of spiritual communication, including prayer, is a major strategy of Satan. Virtually every principle we will discuss can be affected by that reality.

II

THE STILL,
SMALL VOICE
AND INNER NOISE

CHAPTER 4

THE STILL, SMALL VOICE THAT WHISPERS

"Man is apt to look too high or expect too great things so that they often times mistake the Spirit of God and the inspiration of the Almighty. It is not in the thunder or whirlwind that we should look for the Spirit of God but in the still small voice."

—WILFORD WOODRUFF[24]

Hearken to the Voice of the Lord

The opening lines of Doctrine and Covenants, section 1, which the Lord designated as the preface for that book of scripture, contain these words: "Hearken, O ye people of my church, saith the *voice* of him who dwells on high. . . . For verily the *voice of the Lord* is unto all men" (D&C 1:1–2). This declaration boldly refutes the idea common in Christendom that God no longer speaks to His children. The voice of the Lord speaks in our day.

So what is the voice of the Lord like? Is it literally a voice? Can one hear it with his or her ears? Is there something about that voice that helps us distinguish it from other voices? Ancient prophets often indicated when God had spoken to them with, "Thus saith the Lord," or "Thus saith our God." But that is not always the case. It would be foolish to expect that every time God answers one of our prayers, He will preface it with, "Thus saith the Lord." And even though that phrase from both ancient and modern scripture indicates *when* God is speaking, it doesn't tell us *what* the voice of God is actually like.

Fortunately, however, in the Doctrine and Covenants, the Lord has specifically told us what His voice is like: "Thus saith the still small voice, which whispereth through and pierceth all things, and often times it maketh my bones to quake while it maketh manifest" (D&C 85:6).

We learn four important things about the voice of God from this passage:

1. The voice of the Lord is *still*. That sounds like a contradiction. How can a voice be still when the very word implies audible sound? We shall answer that question a little later.

2. The voice of the Lord is *small*. Here is another puzzling word. Normally "small" describes something limited in size,

duration, or number; something trifling or of little significance. None of those seems to fit here. Could it mean something more like "mild" or "pleasant" as opposed to "loud" and "strident"?

3. The voice of the Lord *whispers*. When someone whispers it is usually not just lower in volume. Generally a whisper creates words using one's breath rather than the vocal cords. Thus it is not as distinct as when we are speaking aloud.

4. Even though the voice of the Lord is still, is small, and whispers, its impact on the heart and mind can be deeply powerful. Note how all the elements are described in this passage from the Book of Mormon: "It was not a voice of thunder, neither was it a voice of a great tumultuous noise, but behold, it was a still voice of perfect mildness, as if it had been a whisper, *and it did pierce even to the very soul*" (Helaman 5:30).

President Boyd K. Packer said this about the nature of the voice: "The Spirit does not get our attention by shouting or shaking us with a heavy hand. Rather it whispers. It caresses so gently, that if we are preoccupied, we may not feel it at all. . . . Occasionally it will press just firmly enough for us to pay heed. But most of the time, if we do not heed the gentle feeling, the Spirit will withdraw and wait until we come seeking and listening."[25]

This is very insightful, but not very comforting. The Spirit doesn't work with us as parents do with their children. When parents speak and their children do not respond, they typically initiate escalating levels of response. First, they repeat what they said, raising their voice in volume and sharpness. If there is still no response, they speak even louder, warning of possible consequences for ignoring them. If still nothing happens, parents may take children by the shoulders and shake them gently, saying, "Listen to me!" This is definitely not how the Spirit works with us.

Next, President Packer said that the Spirit *caresses* so gently that if we are preoccupied, we might not hear it at all. Here's another challenge. *Preoccupied?* Whatever would cause us to be preoccupied with things other than communicating with God? Well, here are just a few possibilities: our full-time occupation, cooking three meals a day for our families, cleaning the house, shopping, taking children to the doctor or dentist, an automobile that dies on the freeway, getting a college degree, starting a new business, caring for aged parents, going on vacation, a flooded basement, the wedding of a child, texting and social media, surfing the Internet, playing video games, no paycheck for the last three months, crabgrass in our lawns and termites in our basements, serving faithfully in the Church, etc., etc., etc.

In a word, we are continually preoccupied with *life!* Is it any wonder that sometimes we miss the whisperings of the Spirit?

Another complication is that because the voice of the Lord is still and small and whispers, it is hard to clearly define what it really "sounds" like. President Joseph Fielding Smith said: "There are spiritual influences that are just as deep and meaningful as anything that is tangible to the natural senses; yet they cannot be described or explained. They come through the still small voice of the Spirit. They are penetrating but cannot be described any more than the feelings of love, sympathy, friendship, can be defined and fathomed."[26]

If we have a hard time even defining it, then clearly recognizing and responding to the Spirit can be a problem. And that's only the first problem. President Henry B. Eyring described another: "Your problem and mine is not to get God to speak to us: few of us have reached the point where He has been compelled to turn away from us. *Our problem is to hear.*"[27]

So the first challenge with hearing the voice of the Lord comes from the very nature of the voice. It is still. It is small. And it whispers. Which creates a second challenge: we may not hear it at all.

To the Mind and to the Heart

Another scripture tells us what the voice of the Lord is like and helps us better understand its unique nature: "Yea, behold, I will tell you in your mind and in your heart, by the Holy Ghost, which shall come upon you and which shall dwell in your heart. Now, behold, this is the spirit of revelation" (D&C 8:2–3).

This passage teaches us that the voice speaks to us in two ways:

1. In the *mind*, which represents our intellect. If the Lord chooses to speak to our minds, we would likely say that it comes as *thoughts*.

2. In the *heart*, which represents our emotion. If the Lord chooses to speak to our hearts, we would likely say that it comes as *feelings*.

President Boyd K. Packer said this about the voice of the Lord: "The Holy Ghost communicates with the spirit through the mind more than through the physical senses. This guidance comes as thoughts, as feelings, through impressions and promptings. It is not always easy to describe inspiration. The scriptures teach us that we may 'feel' the words of spiritual communication more than hear them, and see with spiritual rather than with mortal eyes."[28]

Here is yet another challenge: the very nature of human consciousness is that we experience a constant stream of thoughts and feelings. Think about that. Every moment of our waking lives we are like a great river of thoughts and feelings, experiencing a whole gamut of ideas and emotions. So when we pray for help and guidance, if the Lord gives us the answer as a thought or feeling, how do we distinguish it from all the other thoughts and feelings that are an integral part of our daily lives? It shouldn't surprise us that one of the most common questions we ask ourselves when seeking answers from the Lord is, "Was that thought or feeling or impression from the Lord? Or was it just me? Is what I'm feeling right now the answer to my prayers, or just my own emotions? Was that a premonition of danger or just my natural tendency to be too worrisome?"

As President Dallin H. Oaks explained, "In its most familiar forms, revelation comes by means of words or thoughts or feelings communicated to the mind. . . . This is the experience . . . Nephi described when he reminded his wayward brothers that the Lord had spoken to them in a still small voice, but they 'were past feeling' and 'could not feel his words.'"[29]

Perhaps this is the reason why the voice is described as a *still* voice. It rarely comes as audible sounds, so we don't *hear* it with our ears. Rather we *feel* it in our hearts and minds. And if our "spiritual ears" are not tuned properly then we can miss it completely. That may also explain why the voice is described as *small.* These thoughts and feelings are often so natural, so unremarkable, so mild that we miss them. They don't come with ringtones or audible alerts or alarm bells.

President Thomas S. Monson shared an interesting experience from his life that shows how quietly a thought or feeling may come but how important the prompting may be.

He had a close friend who was stricken by cancer to the point that he could no longer walk or stand. He had to

> "If we stop and feel during prayer, we sometimes hear a still small voice, which enters quietly into our mind and heart. It is so simple and so precise that we often pass it by, thinking that it is just our own idea or a passing thought, not revelation. However, as we reconcile these whisperings to what we know to be true, we soon learn to recognize them; and by recognizing them, we become more able to listen carefully."
>
> —JOSEPH B. WIRTHLIN[30]

use a wheelchair, which was very difficult for him because he had been very active throughout his life. Many prayers and priesthood blessings had been given, but he still was confined to a hospital bed.

One afternoon while swimming in a pool as part of his exercise regimen, President Monson had an impression. Notice how he described the prompting as thoughts and feelings: "*Silently,* but ever so clearly, *there came to my mind the thought:* 'Here you swim almost effortlessly, while your friend Stan is unable to move.' I *felt* the prompting: 'Get to the hospital and give him a blessing.' I ceased my swimming, dressed, and hurried to Stan's room at the hospital. His bed was empty. A nurse said he was in his wheelchair at the swimming pool, preparing for therapy. I hurried to the area, and there was Stan, all alone, at the edge of the deeper portion of the pool [where he was contemplating suicide]. We greeted each other and returned to his room, where a priesthood blessing was provided. Slowly but surely, strength and movement returned to Stan's legs. . . . Today one would not know that Stan had lain so close to death and with no hope of recovery. Frequently Stan speaks in church meetings and tells of the goodness of the Lord to him. To some he reveals the dark thoughts of depression that engulfed him that afternoon as he sat in his wheelchair at the edge of the pool, sentenced, it seemed, to a life of despair. He tells how he pondered the alternative. It would be so easy to propel the hated wheelchair into the silent water of the deep pool. Life would then be over. But at that precise moment he saw me, his friend. That day Stan learned literally that we do not walk alone. I too learned a lesson that day: never, never, never postpone a prompting."[31]

An Experience in Listening

A teacher once gave a demonstration on listening that provided some interesting insights into how we can better listen to the voice of the Lord. He gathered several everyday items from around the home or office and placed them where the class members couldn't see them. Then he had them close their eyes and listen as he took out the items. In the quiet room, he stapled a piece of paper, jangled a set of car keys, shook a small container of breath mints, manipulated a set of fingernail clippers, clicked a ballpoint pen, flicked a ping-pong ball softly with his finger, and scraped his fingernail across a cheese grater. He asked the students to try to guess what each sound was.

No one guessed them all correctly. The ones that were guessed correctly were the sounds the students heard most often—the stapler, the car keys, etc. The lesson learned? *The more familiar we are with certain sounds, the easier it is to recognize them when we hear them.*

In the Doctrine and Covenants we get this statement from the Lord: "They who have sought me early shall find rest to their souls" (D&C 54:10). In other words, the more we experience the voice of the Lord, the more likely we are to recognize it when it comes. The earlier we start receiving revelation in our lives, the more familiar the voice becomes to us.

Next the teacher asked the students to once again close their eyes. Then he had them hold perfectly still and listen to the silence. They were to concentrate and see if they heard any sounds they had not noticed before. He gave them thirty seconds. They were amazed at how much "quiet noise" there was in the room—the hum of florescent lights, distant traffic noise, someone walking by in the hallway, the rustle of clothing when someone close by moved.

Two lessons were learned from this second exercise: (1) *When we reduce the noise around us, we hear things we missed before.* (2) *When we concentrate and focus, we hear things we didn't hear before.*

Finally, the teacher tried one more experiment. He played the students about thirty seconds of a piece of classical music. Then he asked them to tell him what they had just heard. Several immediately said, "Music." Others were more specific and identified it as classical music. He then asked if any could identify the composer. Two correctly guessed it was a piece by Ludwig van Beethoven. Then one girl, a music major at the university, said, "It is the first movement of Beethoven's Third Symphony, which is called the *Eroica* symphony." That amazed all of the others, because she was right.

The lesson learned from this exercise: *The more we know and the more experience we have with the principles and patterns of personal revelation, the more we will be able to recognize revelation for what it is, or recognize what is not from the Lord.*

Think for a moment how the lessons learned from this listening experience have direct application to our receiving *and* recognizing answers to our prayers.

A Cautionary Note

Due to the unusual characteristics of the voice of the Lord, which is unlike any other voice on earth, there is a common mistake that even people of faith make from time to time. That mistake is that sometimes God IS answering us, but we are expecting something more dramatic or more sensational than what the Lord chooses to give us, and therefore we miss it and think that there is no answer.

"Many men seem to have no ear for spiritual messages nor comprehension of them when they come in common dress. . . . Expecting the spectacular, one may not be fully alerted to the constant flow of revealed communication."

—SPENCER W. KIMBALL[32]

The scriptures are filled with examples of great miracles, visions of glory, and visitations by angels. These are miraculous manifestations and leave us filled with awe. It is only natural that we might long to have such remarkable spiritual experiences ourselves. Part of that desire stems from the dramatic nature of the manifestation itself. But another reason we long for such things is because when they come, there is no question about "hearing" them. We wouldn't have to ask, "Was that real or not?"

These experiences are real and incredibly important, and great things come from them, but in the flow of revelation from God to man, they are the *rare* exception. In the vast majority of cases, this is not how we receive revelation. The normal way is through the still, small, whispering voice described above.

We must be careful not to covet these more dramatic forms of revelation. Remember, the Lord decides all aspects of revelation, including *how* it is given. It is not our privilege to order up how we want the answer to come.

Here is another important principle of revelation that we often forget: *What* is given to us in a revelation is more significant than *how* it is given. If the Lord sends us a revelation as a quiet thought or a feeling, it may not be as dramatic as an angel appearing in our room, but it is just as valid and significant.

Our expectations of how revelation comes may not be realistic. We sometimes expect something more dramatic, more spectacular, more amazing than how most revelation comes. This mistake happens enough that modern prophets have warned us against it again and again. As Elder David A. Bednar explained: "Receiving a big answer quickly and all at once is possible and, in fact, does occur in some exceptional circumstances. Perhaps we give overmuch emphasis to the miraculous experiences of Joseph in the Sacred Grove, of Paul on the road to Damascus, and of Alma the Younger. If our personal experiences fall short of these well-known and spiritually dramatic examples, then perhaps we believe something is wrong with or lacking in us. I am suggesting that the particular spiritual process evidenced in these three examples . . . is more rare than routine, more the exception than the rule."[33]

SUMMARY

President Packer summed up the nature of the voice of the Spirit in this way: "The Lord communicates with his children here upon the earth: through the still, small voice. . . . That sweet, quiet voice of inspiration that comes more as a feeling than it does as a sound. That process through which pure intelligence can be spoken into the mind and we can know and understand and have witness of spiritual things. The process is not reserved for the prophets alone, but every righteous seeking soul who will qualify and make himself worthy can have that manner of communication, even as a gift."[34]

Here then is our first specific answer to the title question of this book: *It is very possible that God IS answering us, but we don't recognize the answer for what it is because of the uniqueness of His voice or because we expect something more dramatic than He is willing to send us.*

CHAPTER 5

INNER AND OUTER NOISE

"We live in a culture where more and more we are focused on the small, little screen in our hands than we are on the people around us. . . . As amazing as modern technology can be for spreading the message of the gospel of Jesus Christ and helping us stay connected to family and friends, if we are not vigilant in how we use our personal devices, we too can begin to turn inward and forget that the essence of living the gospel is service."

—BONNIE L. OSCARSON[35]

Missing the Daily Miracle

Sometimes there are things of great value in our lives that happen so frequently and are so much a part of our daily experience that we rarely think about their significance. Breathing is one example. Another is eating. We think about food regularly, but only because we get hungry regularly. We give little or no thought to what it takes to grow, process, and distribute food to seven billion people every day. Nor do we often consider the daily miracle that goes on inside our bodies as food is consumed, processed, and turned into nutrients that sustain life. The blessing of food and nourishment is so common to us that we rarely give it conscious thought.

So it is with the voice of the Lord. How often do those who have been given the gift of the Holy Ghost stop to contemplate what it means to have been given the personal companionship of a member of the Godhead? Sometimes we are conscious of His influence and presence, but most of us, more often than not, are totally oblivious to the Holy Ghost fulfilling His functions with us. Here are just a few examples of how that happens:

- While we are struggling to work out a problem or fix a complicated situation, a spark of inspiration comes and we know exactly what to do. We think, "Perfect! Just what I needed," but give no thought to where that enlightenment came from.

- Parents at home watching television or reading suddenly realize that their teenage child is slightly over his or her curfew. They call and remind the child that it is time to come home. Everything seems normal, but unknown to either of them, a situation was developing that could have become a problem. The parents think of it as a normal part of parenting.

- While we are reading the scriptures or preparing a lesson, there comes one of those quiet but startling "Aha!" moments as new insights and deeper understanding come in a single flash of enlightenment. And we think, "I'm grateful I saw that."

Many years ago, a member of the Twelve was meeting with a group of priesthood leaders. When he opened the time for questions, one teacher asked: "The promise of the sacramental prayer is that if we keep our covenants, we can always have His Spirit to be with us. Do you think it is possible for that to happen every day?"

The Apostle smiled and quietly said, "Oh, I think it is more frequent than that, perhaps at times, even every hour of our waking day."

So why aren't we more aware of those times? Why don't we consistently recognize them for the revelatory moments they are?

As discussed in the last chapter, one possible reason is because the voice of the Lord is so unique that we often do not recognize it for what it is when it comes. Another, which we also discussed in the previous chapter, is that we are too busy, and because of that we miss those quiet, less dramatic moments that characterize how the Spirit works with us.

A third common reason we may miss

"I learned . . . that the description of the Holy Ghost as a still, small voice is real. It is poetic, but it is not poetry. Only when my heart has been still and quiet, in submission like a little child, has the Spirit been clearly audible to my heart and mind."

—HENRY B. EYRING[36]

moments of personal inspiration and revelation is that our lives may be cluttered with too much *outer* noise. Once at a family party, the adults were in one room making plans for a major family activity. The children were in the kitchen playing a game with great exuberance and much shouting and laughter. It got to the point that the adults could not hear one another speak. Finally, one of the exasperated parents turned and called, quite sharply, "Children! You are too loud! Take it outside or go downstairs." They did, and the communication between the adults was restored.

ENVELOPES OF NOISE

Test pilots of high performance aircraft often speak of "pushing the envelope" to see what the plane's capabilities are. By "envelope" they mean the normal flight parameters set for an aircraft. To "push the envelope" is to go beyond those parameters. That is a good metaphor that has application to our key question: "Why isn't God answering our prayers?" Satan often tempts us to "push the envelope" in a whole variety of ways. In a positive way, the Lord expects us to do the same. This is how growth occurs.

As electronic devices have shrunk in size and increased in technical sophistication over the last decade or so, we have become a generation with easily accessible and easily portable "noise." We see people engaged fully in all kinds of activities—walking, jogging, cycling,

"The world is so noisy. There are voices everywhere trying to influence us. We all need time to think. We need to drown out the clamor and noise and simply be quiet. We need time to ponder and meditate, and to contemplate the deeper things of life. We need time to read and to immerse ourselves in the thoughts of great minds."

—GORDON B. HINCKLEY[37]

reading, working, playing, hiking, and so on—wearing earphones or earbuds. They carry portable envelopes of noise with them.

We are not suggesting that this is necessarily a bad thing, but if we live in these envelopes of noise virtually every waking hour of our lives, it can directly impact our ability to hear the whisperings of the Spirit.

It is important to note that for our purposes here, "noise" refers not only to literal, audible sounds but also to other distractions. Examples of this kind of noise would include constant texting, following others on social media, video games, television, and other things that can shut out the world around us. These activities are not wrong in and of themselves, only very noisy.

The more serious kinds of sin—such as immorality, infidelity, pornography, dishonesty, greed, cruelty—create tremendous spiritual noise within us. These require repentance and sometimes priesthood intervention to fix. But as noted in the preface, our focus here is on the less obvious sources of spiritual noise, which we may easily miss:

- Studying our scriptures while music is playing or the television is on.
- Carrying on a text conversation during sacrament meeting, sometimes not even pausing during the prayers.
- Gathering with friends but constantly checking our phones, surfing the Internet or browsing social media sites instead of interacting with one another.
- Spending multiple hours a day playing video games.
- Being on a date at a restaurant, both parties on their cell phones and not paying the slightest attention to each other.
- Sitting before the television or the computer, eyes glued to the screen, while our children rage around us.

There is a difference in some of these examples that needs to be noted. All involve outer noise of some kind, but some also involve some moral—or perhaps just downright foolish—behavior that adds additional inner noise. For example, there is nothing wrong with texting itself, but texting during the sacrament prayer is spiritually deadening. Watching TV is not inherently wrong (again, depending on the content), but it can be a major distraction for someone supposedly trying to study the scriptures. The point is that sometimes we need to tune down or shut off outer noise so that we have quiet time to receive the answers to our prayers that we are seeking (and may be receiving but are not hearing).

President James E. Faust, formerly of the First Presidency, spoke of this "affliction" of spiritual noise in our generation: "The adversary tries to smother this voice with a multitude of loud, persistent, persuasive, and appealing voices: murmuring voices which conjure up perceived injustices; whining voices that abhor challenge and work; seductive voices offering sensual enticements; soothing voices that lull us into carnal security; intellectual voices that profess sophistication and superiority; proud voices that rely on the arm of flesh; flattering voices that puff us up with pride; cynical voices that destroy hope; entertaining voices that promote pleasure seeking; commercial voices which tempt us to 'spend money for that which is of no worth,' and 'labor for that which cannot satisfy.'"[38]

President Thomas S. Monson gave a similar warning: "Now, a word of caution to all—both young and old, both male and female. We live at a time when the adversary is using every means possible to ensnare us in his web of deceit, trying desperately to take us down with him. . . . I feel to mention one in particular, and that is the Internet. On one hand, it provides nearly limitless opportunities for acquiring useful and important information. Through it we can communicate with others around the world. The Church itself has a wonderful Web site, filled with valuable and uplifting information and priceless resources. On the other hand, however—and extremely alarming—are the reports of the number of individuals who are utilizing the Internet for evil and degrading purposes."[39]

PONDER, REFLECT, MEDITATE

One of the marvelous things about the scriptures is that they contain patterns that, when viewed together, open up deeper levels of meaning for the reader. Here is a pattern that teaches us something very significant about how to receive revelation. It involves three different prophets who had marvelous manifestations given to them. The pattern is found in what they were doing just before the manifestations came.

The following table includes (1) Who experienced the revelation, (2) What he was doing at the time he experienced it, and (3) The results. Watch for patterns in each example:

WHO	DOING WHAT	RESULTS	REFERENCE
Nephi	Thinking about the words of his father; he *believed* them and *desired* to see what Lehi had seen; he *pondered* in his heart.	He was caught away in the Spirit and shown a grand vision of the future of his people and the world.	1 Nephi 11:1
Joseph Smith	He *desired* to know which church was right; *serious reflection, deep feelings*; read the words of James; *reflected* on them again and again.	Went to the Grove to pray; saw God and Christ; opened up a new dispensation and restored the Church.	JS—H 1:9–12

WHO	DOING WHAT	RESULTS	REFERENCE
Joseph Smith and Sidney Rigdon	Being *in the Spirit; puzzled* by the words of John 5:29; they *marveled; they meditated* upon them.	The eyes of their understanding were opened; they saw in vision the three degrees of glory.	D&C 76:11–12, 15–19
Joseph F. Smith	Alone in his room, *pondering* over the words of Peter; *reflecting* on Christ's atoning sacrifice; *pondering* over what was written.	The eyes of his understanding were opened; the Spirit of the Lord rested upon him; saw a vision of the spirit world.	D&C 138: 1–2, 11

Note that these men were all in quiet places. In three cases, they were alone. In the other, Joseph Smith and Sidney Rigdon were in a room in the John Johnson home. A few others were in the room with them but did not speak.

Each was reading (or in Nephi's case, remembering) the words of prophets—Lehi, James, John, and Peter.

They came with faith, believing the words of the prophets.

They did more than just read the words. They pondered, meditated, and reflected on them again and again.

Then, in each case, a great spiritual experience followed.

What do we learn from this pattern? It is pretty simple. And it has to do with the concept of "outer noise," which is so much a part of our modern lives. The first step is to turn off the television or radio or electronic device. Next, we find a quiet, private place and carefully study the words of God's prophets, doing so with faith and a desire to gain understanding. Third, we ponder, reflect, and meditate on what we have read, praying for the Spirit to be our companion. Then the eyes of our understanding will be opened, and we will not only get an answer to our prayers, but we will be more likely to recognize it when it comes.

There's the pattern, and reducing the outer noise is a critical part of that pattern.

SUMMARY

In this modern world of ours, noise and distractions come at us in a constant stream. As we noted earlier, personal revelation does not come with audible notifications, ringtones, or beeps to alert us that we have a message. The voice of the Lord is still, it's small, and it whispers. If we are immersed in the roar of the world around us, it's pretty hard to hear a whisper.

Why isn't God answering me?

Maybe He is, but we don't hear His voice when we are enclosed in bubbles of noise. Perhaps this is why the Lord commands us to "Be still and know that I am God" (D&C 101:16).

CHAPTER 6

WE ARE TOO BUSY OR TOO PREOCCUPIED

———⁂———

"We need at times to strive to focus on the basic purposes of our work so that mere 'busy-ness' does not create the illusion that we are effective when we are not."

—SPENCER W. KIMBALL[40]

"FATHER WAS SO BUSY"

Many years ago, President Harold B. Lee spoke to a group of seminary and institute faculty. He shared with them an experience that President David O. McKay had shared with the Twelve the previous day.

"[President McKay] said it is a great thing to be responsive to the whisperings of the Spirit, and we know that when these whisperings come it is a gift and our privilege to have them. They come when we are relaxed and not under pressure of appointments. . . . The President then took occasion to relate an experience in the life of Bishop John Wells, former member of the Presiding Bishopric.

"A son of Bishop Wells was killed in Emigration Canyon on a railroad track. . . . His boy was run over by a freight train. Sister Wells was inconsolable. She mourned during the three days prior to the funeral, received no comfort at the funeral, and was in a rather serious state of mind.

"One day soon after the funeral services while she was lying on her bed relaxed, still mourning, she said her son appeared to her and said, 'Mother, do not mourn, do not cry. I am all right.' He told her that she did not understand how the accident happened and explained that he had given the signal to the engineer to move on, and then made the usual effort to catch the railing on the freight train; but as he attempted to do so his foot caught on a root and he failed to catch the handrail, and his body fell under the train. It was clearly an accident.

"Now, listen. He said that as soon as he realized that he was in another environment he tried to see his father, but couldn't reach him. His father was so busy with the duties in his office he could not respond to his call. Therefore he had come to his mother. He said to her, 'You tell Father that all is well with me, and I want you not to mourn anymore.'"[41]

What makes this such a powerful lesson for our purposes is that Bishop Wells was not some business tycoon, utterly consumed with making millions of dollars. It wasn't as though he were out playing golf or taking a cruise. There was no sinful or inappropriate behavior. He was Second Counselor in the Presiding Bishopric, a General Authority in the Church. And he was at his office, doing the work of the kingdom.

What a wonderful, comforting blessing it was for this highly distraught mother to have her son appear to her and assure her that he was all right. But think for a moment how Bishop Wells must have felt when his wife told him what his son had said: "Father was so busy he could not respond to my call." A visit from a loved one from the spirit world is a rare and marvelous experience, and Bishop Wells missed it because he was too busy.

Here is a source of "inner noise" that can be easily overlooked but that can still drown out the still, small voice. Though we may not think of it as having an effect on personal revelation and getting answers to our prayers, it can cause us to miss opportunities to receive spiritual enlightenment.

OF SEEDS, SOILS, AND HEARTS

Early in His ministry, Jesus taught the multitude a parable about a sower out in his field planting grain. Even the Twelve and the inner circle of the Savior's disciples were puzzled by this new approach in His teachings. So later, when they were alone with Him, they asked Jesus to help them understand its meaning (see Matthew 13; Mark 4; Luke 8).

Jesus explained that the seed in the parable represented the word of God—the gospel of Jesus Christ. The sower represented Jesus Himself and anyone else who spreads the gospel to the world. The seed fell on four different kinds of soil. Jesus likened that soil to the heart, particularly in its readiness to receive the word (see Matthew 13:19–23).

Though there were four types of soil in the parable, in this chapter we are going to focus on only one of them: that which Jesus described as "thorny ground." Bible scholars think "thorns" refer to both thorn bushes and what we call thistles. Both plants grow in wild abundance in the Holy Land. They can grow so thick that even a horse cannot push through a field of them. Because they grow so close together, no other plants can thrive among them. Note that in this case, the soil itself (the heart) is good soil; otherwise the thorns would not grow so abundantly there. The problem is not the heart itself but what is allowed to grow in the heart along with the seed of the word of God.

This parable is recorded by Matthew, Mark, and Luke. The three authors reported Jesus' explanation of what the thorny ground represented with slight variations. These variations are helpful, for they give us a fuller picture of what Jesus was trying to teach. Here are their accounts of what Jesus said the thorny ground represents:

"The *care of this world*, and the *deceitfulness of riches*" (Matthew 13:22).

"The *cares of this world*, and *the deceitfulness of riches*, and the *lusts of other things*" (Mark 4:19). (Note: "lusts" as used here does not mean only sexual appetites. The definition includes desires, cravings, or longings.)

"Choked with *cares* and *riches* and *pleasures of this life*" (Luke 8:14).

In the last chapter we used the metaphor of inner noise to give one possible explanation for why we may not be getting answers to our prayers. Here is another possible reason.

THE CARES OF THIS WORLD

In English, we often use the word *care* in the sense of concern, love, or affection. But that is not the basic meaning of the word. The Greek word used in the New Testament means *anxiety*, and that comes much closer to its original meaning in English as well. Care is defined as "a state of mind in which one is troubled; [or has] worry, anxiety, concern and grief."[42]

When things in life are going well, we often say, "I don't have a care in the world." Clearly that cannot be taken literally, but it does convey that, for the moment at least, things are good, that we are not burdened with the troubles of life. This definition of *care* is important as we search for things that may be choking out the spiritual or making it more difficult to recognize answers to prayers when they come.

As Jesus explained to His disciples, the thorns and thistles represented three things: *riches,* the *pleasures of life,* and *lusting for* (or craving) *the things of the world.* Any one of these three "heart problems" can lead us into full-blown sin and wickedness. For example, the "pleasures of the world" may at first conjure up in our minds the concept of sexual immorality in all of its various forms. But reading a good book or listening to good music can also be one of the simple pleasures of life. Surely raising a happy and righteous family qualifies for that title. We can crave a good education,

> *"Isn't it true that we often get so busy? And, sad to say, we even wear our busyness as a badge of honor, as though being busy, by itself, was an accomplishment or sign of a superior life. Is it?"*
>
> —DIETER F. UCHTDORF[43]

excellence in some aspect of our lives, or trustworthy friends who will encourage us in our efforts.

But here, we are looking for those worries, anxieties, and griefs that can create spiritual noise in our lives or conceal the reasons our prayers are not being answered. We note again that these may not be inherently evil things, but when they grow too thick in our hearts, they can inhibit the flow of inspiration.

Here are just a few examples of things that would qualify as the cares of this world and could create sufficient inner noise to make it difficult for us to hear the voice of the Lord or receive answers to our earnest prayers:

- Being a parent with young, highly active, demanding children.
- Being a student cramming for final exams.
- Having to work two or three jobs in order to support a family.
- Facing serious mental or physical challenges.
- Serving as a bishop in a large ward.
- Having a tight deadline on a major project at work.
- Facing a lawsuit that threatens financial ruin.
- Being unemployed for months and seeing no apparent solution in sight.
- Being the primary caregiver for a family member who is suffering from long-term illness.
- Having a child who has left the Church.
- Experiencing the constant hardship of lifelong poverty.

All of these things, and countless other cares of the world, place huge demands on us. They leave us mentally, emotionally, and spiritually drained. They rob us of sleep. They create ulcers and other health problems. They can siphon off enormous amounts of our financial resources. And, most discouraging of all, in many cases there seems to be no solution, no way out, and a pall of hopelessness descends upon us. No wonder that at times we feel like we are minuscule grains of wheat in some grand, relentless gristmill or the rocks at the base of a three-hundred-foot waterfall. It is no surprise that we begin to wonder if God has abandoned us—and if so, why?

Is There a Solution Out There?

So let's discuss some possible solutions. As we do so, let us remember that what we need here may be a reordering of our priorities more than just a change of routine. Or it may be that what is needed is simply an injection of strength and hope to endure what we are facing. In some cases the solution may be something as simple as finding an hour or so of quiet time. In more dramatic circumstances, where finding time to push back the busyness is very difficult, we cannot wait to *find* time for these more important things. We may have to *make* time to simplify our lives.

"Are there so many fascinating, exciting things to do or so many challenges pressing down upon you that it is hard to keep focused on that which is essential? When things of the world crowd in, all too often the wrong things take highest priority. Then it is easy to forget the fundamental purpose of life. Satan has a powerful tool to use against good people. It is distraction. He would have good people fill life with 'good things' so there is no room for the essential ones. Have you unconsciously been caught in that trap?"

—Richard G. Scott[44]

Here are three ways we can reduce the inner noise of busyness and the cares of the world:

1. *Carefully evaluate your priorities.* In general conference in 2007, President Dallin H. Oaks gave a wonderful talk titled "Good,

Better, Best." It was a thoughtful and balanced call for wisdom when our lives grow overly complicated and encumbered. He suggested that we begin by recognizing the reality that just because something is good is not a sufficient reason for doing it. As he said, "The number of good things we can do far exceeds the time available to accomplish them. Some things are better than good, and these are the things that should command priority attention in our lives."

President Oaks went on to teach: "In choosing how we spend time as a family, we should be careful not to exhaust our available time on things that are merely good and leave little time for that which is better or best. . . . Super family activities may be good for children, but they are not always better than one-on-one time with a loving parent. The amount of children-and-parent time absorbed in the good activities of private lessons, team sports, and other school and club activities also needs to be carefully regulated. . . . Parents should act to preserve time for family prayer, family scripture study, family home evening, and the other precious togetherness and individual one-on-one time that binds a family together and fixes children's values on things of eternal worth. . . . Church leaders should be aware that Church meetings and activities can become too complex and burdensome if a ward or a stake tries to have the membership do everything that is good and possible in our numerous Church programs. Priorities are needed there also."[45]

A poetess, who is clearly a mother, too, penned this simple but profound reminder:

> *Cleaning and scrubbing can wait 'til tomorrow.*
> *For babies grow up, we've learned to our sorrow.*
> *So quiet down cobwebs, dust go to sleep.*
> *I'm rocking my baby, and babies don't keep.*
>
> —Ruth Hurlburt Hamilton

2. *Slow down!* One of the first assignments I had after being called to serve as a General Authority Seventy was to accompany President Boyd K. Packer, the President of the Quorum of the Twelve Apostles, to a regional training session for stake presidencies. After some preliminary talks, President Packer spoke briefly to those present and then opened the meeting for questions. One stake president asked: "President Packer, you've been in the leading councils of the Church for almost forty years now. What advice would you give us on how to be more effective priesthood leaders?"

President Packer nodded thoughtfully and then told them that his first suggestion was to slow down! That obviously startled the group, so he went on to say that as stake presidencies, they were so busy in their Church callings, occupational demands, and family obligations, that they sometimes were "too busy" for revelation. Then he said, "Remember, brethren, you will get more revelation on your knees than you will in a meeting."

Here is more prophetic counsel on this subject. Before telling his people of the numerous ways we can sin, King Benjamin gave this interesting counsel to his people: "And see that all these things are done *in wisdom and order; for it is not requisite that a man should run faster than he has strength.* And again, it is expedient that he should be diligent, that thereby he might win the prize; therefore, all things must be done in order" (Mosiah 4:27).

After Joseph Smith lost the 116 pages of Book of Mormon manuscript, the Lord gave him similar counsel: "Do not run faster or labor more than you have strength and means provided" (D&C 10:4).

This is a good question to ask ourselves. "Am I at a point where I am running faster than I have strength? Could that be why I am always so exhausted?" If that is the case, how do we not run faster than we have strength? One way is to slow down.

Another is to eliminate those things that are of lower value in our lives where necessary. Sister Carol F. McConkie, First Counselor in the Young Women General Presidency, said: "If we would be holy, we must learn to sit at the feet of the Holy One of Israel and give time to holiness. Do we set aside the phone, the never-ending to-do list, and the cares of worldliness? Prayer, study, and heeding the word of God invite His cleansing and healing love into our souls. Let us take time to be holy, that we may be filled with His sacred and sanctifying Spirit."[46]

When the cares of the world press in, and our anxiety deepens, and our frustrations multiply, and it feels as if there is no possible way we will ever cross the finish line, what do we do? Slow down! Simplify! Prioritize!

The Lord, who knows us far better than we know ourselves, perfectly understands our limitations. This counsel from Him is not only good counsel for our mental and spiritual health, but it blesses us in another critical way. It reduces the clutter and busyness of our lives and makes it more likely that we will hear His answers when we cry to Him for help.

No, we're not talking about simple solutions here, because so much of what is cluttering our lives are good things—things we want for ourselves and our children, and often things we cannot neglect. But that doesn't alter the fact that the "good" thorns of life are choking out the "best" things. And these two concepts coupled together—reordering our priorities and slowing down—will go a long way in reducing the spiritual noise in our lives. As the prophet Jacob taught so many years ago, "O be wise; what can I say more?" (Jacob 6:12).

3. *Pray.* Guess what immediately followed the Lord's counsel

to Joseph to not run faster than he had strength? "Pray always, that you may come off conqueror" (D&C 10:5). The placement of those two concepts together doesn't seem accidental. It is ironic that as we increasingly complicate our lives, prayer is often one of the first things to be compromised. Our prayers grow shorter, terser, and less frequent.

While we are expected to use our own best judgment and good old common sense in simplifying our complex and cluttered lives, let us not forget that the Lord offers to help us do so wisely. There are many places where He invites us to pray, but to Joseph Smith He tied prayer directly to His caution not to run faster than he had strength. So as we undertake an effort to simplify and quiet our lives, why not start with prayer?

But, by the way, don't be surprised if His answer doesn't come after the first prayer. And don't be surprised if His answer is not what you hoped it would be. Or if He asks you to eliminate something you're doing that you love a great deal. Or if His answer is, "Sorry, but this burden is going to remain with you right now. But fear not. I will strengthen and enable you to move forward."

Remember this promise from the Lord: "If men come unto me I will show unto them their weakness. I give unto men weakness that they may be humble; and *my grace is sufficient for all men that humble themselves before me;* for if they humble themselves before me, and have faith in me, *then will I make weak things become strong unto them*" (Ether 12:27).

SUMMARY

One of my favorite artistic renderings of our Savior is the one where He is standing beneath a tree beside a stone wall. Directly in front of Him there is a simple wooden door, and He is knocking on it.

This painting is based on a scripture in the book of Revelation. The verse contains the words of the Savior Himself: "I stand at the door, and knock: if any man hear my voice, and open the door, I will come in to him, and will sup with him, and he with me" (Revelation 3:20).

It is a lovely invitation from the Savior to His disciples. But on closer examination of the painting, we notice an oddity. There is no door latch on the door, no handle. It must be opened from the inside. That is significant. The Savior doesn't say, "I am standing behind the door waiting for you. When you knock, then I will open the door."

No. It is the other way around. He is the one who knocks. His invitation has already been extended to us. Now He is waiting for us to respond. How sad will we be if it turns out that we were so busy with other things that we didn't even know that He was there? What if we are so burdened by the cares of the world that we don't hear the knock at all?

When we cry, "Why isn't God answering me?" let us be sure that the answer is not, "I *am* answering, but your life is so frenetic, so encumbered and busy, that spiritual things are being choked out and you don't hear when I speak to you."

CHAPTER 7

THE SPIRIT OF CONTENTION

———— ✑ ————

"When there is contention, the Spirit of the Lord will depart, regardless of who is at fault."

—JAMES E. FAUST[47]

"THE SPIRIT OF CONTENTION IS NOT OF ME"

The resurrected Christ came to the land of Bountiful to visit the more righteous part of the Nephites, those who had been spared from the great destruction. What followed for those gathered there at the temple was an experience the likes of which few others in all of human history have experienced. A multitude of about 2,500 were allowed to come forward one by one and feel the wounds He had received during His Crucifixion (see 3 Nephi 11:14).

When all had passed by Him, the Savior brought Nephi and eleven others forward and called them to lead the Church in the Americas. He also gave them the power and authority to baptize people into the Church. This was in prelude to an extensive period of teaching the people directly. But before beginning that general teaching experience, the Savior taught this important principle to the Twelve: "There shall be no disputations among you, as there have hitherto been; neither shall there be disputations among you concerning the points of my doctrine, as there have hitherto been. For verily, verily I say unto you, *he that hath the spirit of contention is not of me,* but is of the devil, who is the father of contention, and *he stirreth up the hearts of men to contend with anger, one with another*" (3 Nephi 11:28–29).

Some of these disputations seem to have arisen over questions concerning baptism. We're not told how widespread the contention was, but before proceeding any further, Jesus felt compelled to counsel these fledgling leaders of His Church to be sure it was eliminated.

Note that Jesus didn't just condemn angry disagreement, but the "*spirit* of contention," saying, it "is not of me." *Spirit* here seems to imply a disposition to be disagreeable—something that is more habitual. We call such people "contentious."

President Dallin H. Oaks defined the essence of what is meant by a spirit of contention: "It is necessary to emphasize that the kind of contention discussed in this chapter is synonymous with wrath, strife, angry disputes, and quarreling. This is the meaning expressed in the adjective contentious. Holding different views or conversing about points of disagreement does not constitute this kind of contention. Neither does an argument or a debate, if (a big if) it can be done with a peaceful spirit and method. In short, the kind of contention treated here consists of disagreement plus a wrathful spirit or a quarrelsome method."[48]

Contention is another type of behavior that we may easily overlook as we are taking inventory of the possible reasons we are not getting answers to our prayers. Many would agree that contention is a weakness but would not think of it as a serious sin. But surely, if Jesus so roundly condemned contention, we should assume that it can have a toxic effect on our sensitivity to the Spirit.

Another indicator of the seriousness of contention is "the company it keeps." Note some of the companions of contention found in the scriptures: contention and war (see Omni 1:10); contention and dissension (see Words of Mormon 1:16); contention and the shedding of blood (see Mosiah 29:21); contention and disturbance (see Alma 22:22); contention and lack of peace (see Alma 50:25); contention and taking up arms (see Alma 50:26); contention and difficulties (see Helaman 1:18); contention and pride (see Helaman 3:1); contention and wickedness (see 3 Nephi 7:7); contention and strife (see Proverbs 17:14); contention and iniquity and violence (see Habakkuk 1:3).

These accompanying conditions are hardly the "company" we desire in our lives, and they certainly are not qualities associated with the Holy Ghost.

"Cease to Contend One with Another"

Jesus taught that contention is of the devil. This makes sense because, as we said early on, one of Satan's prime strategic objectives is to disrupt the lines of communication between us and God, including the process of prayer. So it should not surprise us that he uses the weaknesses and flaws of human nature to stir up contention. And unfortunately, one of the fertile seedbeds he finds for this kind of behavior is the family. Best friends can also get caught up in it. All too often we find it occurring in those with believing hearts. Amiable disagreements or differences of opinions suddenly become something that we feel we have to defend at all costs. Our voices rise in volume, and amiability quickly evaporates as pride kicks in and becomes the driver. Missionary companionships are a prime target for the evil one because contention quenches the Spirit so effectively. Sometimes we see it erupt in Church classes or quorums. Church sports events quickly get out of hand. We find it in the workplace or at school. And sometimes, emotions boil over and verbal conflict turns into physical violence. Ironically, when things calm down again, sometimes the disputants can't even remember what started the argument in the first place.

President Russell M. Nelson said: "Contention is becoming accepted as a way of life. From what we see and hear in the media, the classroom, and the workplace, all are now infected to some degree

> *"The moment that a Latter-day Saint learns his duty, he will learn that it is his business to make peace, to establish good will, to work righteousness, to be filled with the spirit of kindness, love, charity, and forgiveness; and, so far as he is concerned, there can be no war, no strife, no contention, no quarreling, no disunion."*
>
> —Spencer W. Kimball[49]

with contention. How easy it is, yet how wrong it is, to allow habits of contention to pervade matters of spiritual significance, because contention is forbidden by divine decree."[50]

CONTENTION IN THE FAMILY

A simple definition of a family is a group consisting of parents and children living together in a household. A more accurate (but tongue-in-cheek) description might go something like this: a group of widely different individuals who are bound together by ties of blood or adoption, who are living in the same home, sharing the same limited space, eating the same daily food, sharing (or avoiding) the same household duties, jointly draining the same limited financial resources, and who are emotionally tied together in a curious balance of mutual love and frequent emotional combat.

If we are examining ourselves to see if contention could be one of the reasons we are not getting answers to our prayers, a good place to start is in our own families. It is a rare family that is free of conflicts and disagreements. That is to be expected, though that doesn't make it all right. But unfortunately, these patterns of disagreement can easily become habitual and too often morph into patterns of contention. In a public setting, a father proudly said that in his family, never an unkind word was spoken between husband and wife, between parent and child, or between siblings. Someone who knew the family well quipped, "Either his memory is slipping, his hearing is fading, his perception of reality is seriously lacking, or he is never at home."

It is only natural that there will be differences and disagreements, competition and criticism, hard feelings and hurt egos, and vigorous debates on the merits of different alternatives. And, as

President Oaks said above, that is not what creates the problems with the Spirit. Problems occur when the complicated dynamics of family interactions get out of hand and contention becomes a norm. Then reason and kindness and respect for one another's opinions are pushed back as each strives to prove that he or she is right or desires to hurt and shame an opponent.

This is not just a modern phenomenon. Over two thousand years ago, King Benjamin counseled his people (who had just covenanted to become the children of Christ) on being good parents, saying, "Ye will not suffer your children that they go hungry, or naked; neither will ye suffer that they transgress the laws of God, *and fight and quarrel one with another,* and serve the devil, who is the master of sin" (Mosiah 4:14).

That is the key. Disagreements occur naturally, but do we let them escalate into full-scale and habitual contention, or do we step in and teach and counsel and adjudicate so that our children don't develop a habit of contentiousness? And do we examine our own patterns and make changes where necessary?

There is a wonderful example of this from the early history of the Church. While he was working on the translation of the Book of Mormon, Joseph Smith had many distractions, some of which clearly fit into the category of "the cares of this world" described in Chapter 6. He had to stop work on the translation from time to time to take care of his financial needs, even though he was receiving help from loyal supporters. Emma had lost a baby and was in very frail health. There was tension between Emma's parents and Joseph because he refused to let them see the gold plates. And, as always, his enemies were constantly hounding him. The work was accelerated when Oliver Cowdery came to Harmony, Pennsylvania, and became Joseph's scribe. Then, through Oliver's influence,

Joseph, Emma, and Oliver were invited to move to Fayette, New York, and live with Peter Whitmer Sr. and his family.

Sometime while Joseph and Emma were there, an incident occurred that shows how delicate our spiritual sensors are. The account was written by David Whitmer later in his life: "One morning when [Joseph] was getting ready to continue the translation, something went wrong about the house and he was put out about it. Something that Emma, his wife, had done. Oliver and I went up stairs and Joseph came up soon after to continue the translation, but he could not do anything. He could not translate a single syllable. He went down stairs, out into the orchard, and made supplication to the Lord; was gone about an hour—he came back to the house, asked Emma's forgiveness and then came up stairs where we were and the translation went on all right."[51]

This doesn't seem to have been some major blowup or some ongoing, long-lasting contention between them. But even if it was nothing more than a flash of irritation, a brief loss of temper that caused a few unkind words to pass between them, it was enough to throw Joseph off his stride when he tried to translate.

Three things happened in that healing process. First, Joseph felt sorrow for what he had done. Next, there was confession of wrongdoing (perhaps on both of their parts), and finally forgiveness was extended. These actions were born out of Joseph and Emma's love for and commitment to each other. This is a wonderful model for us on how to overcome contention in our homes.

President Ezra Taft Benson gave a simple but very practical

"Contention in our families drives the Spirit of the Lord away. It also drives many of our family members away. Contention ranges from a hostile spoken word to worldwide conflicts."

—Ezra Taft Benson[52]

piece of counsel for those who wish to reduce contention in their homes: "I feel certain that if, in our homes, parents will read from the Book of Mormon prayerfully and regularly, both by themselves and with their children, the spirit of that great book will come to permeate our homes and all who dwell therein. The spirit of reverence will increase; mutual respect and consideration for each other will grow. *The spirit of contention will depart.* Parents will counsel their children in greater love and wisdom. Children will be more responsive and submissive to that counsel. Righteousness will increase. Faith, hope, and charity—the pure love of Christ—will abound in our homes and lives, bringing in their wake peace, joy, and happiness."[53]

"Words have surprising power, both to build up and to tear down. We can all probably remember negative words that brought us low and other words spoken with love that made our spirits soar. Choosing to say only that which is positive about— and to—others lifts and strengthens those around us and helps others follow in the Savior's way."

—JEAN B. BINGHAM[54]

SUMMARY

Since contention, especially in its lesser forms, is so common, it is another example of behavior that can create enough inner noise to explain why we're not getting answers or not recognizing them when they come, even though we may be doing many other things right.

As we wrestle with the question of whether contention is a possible reason God isn't answering us, consider this wise counsel from President Russell M. Nelson: "Prior to His ascension from the Holy Land, the Savior pronounced a unique blessing: 'Peace I leave with you, my peace I give unto you: not as the world giveth, give I unto you.' His peace is not necessarily political; His peace is personal. But that spirit of inner peace is driven away by contention. . . . As we dread any disease that undermines the health of the body, so should we deplore contention, which is a corroding canker of the spirit. . . . What can we do to combat this canker of contention? What steps may each of us take to supplant the spirit of contention with a spirit of personal peace? To begin, show compassionate concern for others. Control the tongue, the pen, and the word processor. . . . Bridle the passion to speak or write contentiously for personal gain or glory. . . . Such high mutual regard would then let us respectfully disagree without being disagreeable. . . . Personal peace is reached when one, in humble submissiveness, truly loves God. Heed carefully this scripture: '*There was no contention in the land, because of the love of God which did dwell in the hearts of the people.*'"[55]

CHAPTER 8

OUR WANTS ARE TOO HIGH

———✦———

"The Lord has His own timetable. . . . The first principle of the gospel is faith in the Lord Jesus Christ. Faith means trust—trust in God's will, trust in His way of doing things, and trust in His timetable. We should not try to impose our timetable on His. Indeed, we cannot have true faith in the Lord without also having complete trust in the Lord's will and in the Lord's timing."

—DALLIN H. OAKS[56]

EMOTIONAL NOISE

How often in our lifetimes have we experienced something like this: Our families are getting ready to leave on an extended vacation. Everything is packed and loaded into the vehicle. The kids are sent off to the bathroom one last time while Mom and Dad go through the house—again!—to check that all the windows and the doors are locked. Finally, with everyone stuffed in the car, we drive off with a huge sigh of relief.

Then, about ten minutes down the road, someone (often the mother) suddenly jerks to attention and says, "Did I leave the iron on?" (Or the stove, or the oven, or something else equally critical.) We're pretty sure we didn't, but we're not positive, and we wonder if maybe this is the Spirit prompting us that we left a dangerous situation behind. So we turn around and go back. And when we get back in the house and check the iron, not only do we find that it was *not* on, but then we remember that we checked it twice before we left!

So, how can we tell if these kinds of feelings are actual warnings or promptings from the Holy Ghost or if they are just our own natural tendency to fret and worry? And if it is our own tendency to worry, why doesn't the Lord set up a system for us to clearly distinguish between true revelation and our own emotion? Alas, that is not His way. Remember what President Packer said about counterfeit

"The adversary is delighted when we act like sightseers, meaning those who are hearers rather than doers of the word, or shoppers, meaning those preoccupied with the vain things of this world that suffocate our spirits. Satan baits us with perishable pleasures and preoccupations—our bank accounts, our wardrobes, even our waistlines—for he knows that where our treasure is, there will our hearts be also."

—SHERI DEW[57]

revelation in Chapter 3: "The spiritual part of us and the emotional part of us are so closely linked, it is possible to mistake an emotional impulse for something spiritual."[58] It is safe to assume that we could turn that last sentence around and say, "It is also possible to mistake a true spiritual prompting for our own emotional impulse."

This is one of the ancillary aspects of the unique nature of the Lord's voice. As often as not, it is not easily recognized. When it comes to getting answers to our prayers, one of the most frequent questions we ask is, "How can I tell if that was from the Lord or if it was just me?"

Here are three ways that our emotions can confuse us about personal revelation:

1. We want something so badly that it tends to dominate our thoughts and feelings, making it difficult for us to put our will in subjection to His or making it so that we don't recognize the voice of the Lord when He does speak to us.
2. We believe that having strong feelings proves that these feelings come from God.
3. We become self-centered and selfish, putting our needs, wants, desires, and priorities ahead of those of others, sometimes including God, and this deadens our spiritual senses.

Pushing Down Our Desires

We have all watched young children see something in a store that catches their eye and beg their parents to buy it for them. It is the coolest, most desirable thing in the world ever, and if they don't have it they shall surely die right on the spot. But if the parents hold firm and say no, the children miraculously manage to survive, and a minute or two later, they see something else, and the scene is repeated. Only this time, it *really* is the coolest thing ever and they *really* will die if they don't get it.

Unfortunately, as adults, we don't always fully grow out of that mode. We too may want something so badly that we press for our own desires rather than what the Lord wants for us. Consider some "grown-up" examples of this behavior:

- We run up enormous credit card debt because we see something, we want it, and we buy it.
- A couple foregoes spending money on an enriching class, saying they don't have the money. Two weeks later they go on a shopping spree at the mall.
- A son gives a blessing to his father, who is suffering from terminal cancer. The son promises him that he will live for several more years. Within the week, the father passes away.
- A missionary is insistent that he go home. When asked what he will do when he returns, he answers that he hasn't made any goals or plans.
- A spouse who was married in the temple feels strong attraction for someone besides his or her spouse and claims that the Spirit is guiding him or her to leave the marriage and begin a new relationship.
- A young married couple feels a strong spiritual prompting to begin growing their family, but after talking it through they decide they are not financially or professionally prepared to have children and so do not act on the prompting.

STRONG FEELINGS ARE NOT ENOUGH

It is not uncommon to hear people testify that they received an answer to their prayers and that they know it was from God because they "felt so strongly about it." Here too we must take care. Undoubtedly, there are times when revelation comes in strong and dramatic ways. But to set strong feelings up as the test for whether our feelings and thoughts are from the Lord can be highly problematic. We feel strongly about all kinds of things that are not necessarily good.

For example, a young man, pressing his girlfriend to go further than she feels comfortable with, cries out in exasperation when she tells him to stop, "This feels *so* right! It can't be wrong!" Think how often strong feelings of attraction or greed or religious fervor can lead to immorality, divorce, crime, and even heinous atrocities supposedly done in the name of God. Jesus warned the Twelve in the Upper Room the night before His death that the time would come when "whosoever killeth you will think that he doeth God service" (John 16:2).

Here is some wise counsel from President Henry B. Eyring: "I have had prayers answered. Those answers were most clear *when what I wanted was silenced by an overpowering need to know what God wanted.* It is then that the answer from a loving Heavenly Father can be spoken to the mind by the still, small voice and can be written in the heart."[59]

SELFISHNESS

One common denominator in both of the topics we have discussed so far in this chapter is selfishness, or being self-centered. Why would a missionary choose to return home early with no other plans or goals? Because his personal wants and desires for comfort took priority over everything else. Why does a boy press a girl to go further in their physical affection than is comfortable? Well, in spite of what he says, it is not his tender love for her that's motivating him!

Again we note that in several of these examples, we are not talking about glaring, terrible sins. Many times the instances of selfishness are not obvious things that we would associate with not getting answers to prayers. We are not talking about wicked people here. Here are two actual examples of petty selfishness that can still have detrimental effects:

One roommate ate her roommate's food without permission, and then when she was confronted about it, she became huffy and said, "I was hungry, and there was nothing else to eat," as if that were the perfect justification. No apology. No remorse.

> *"The element of selfishness crowds in upon us constantly. We need to overcome it, and there is no better way than to go to the house of the Lord and there serve in a vicarious relationship in behalf of those who are beyond the veil of death."*
>
> —Gordon B. Hinckley[60]

Another young adult moved into his two-person apartment and found that all of the bookshelf space was already full. When he pointed out to his roommate that it was designed for each person to have half of the shelf, the roommate's reply was, "So? I'm a sophomore. You're a freshman. And besides, I got here first. Don't make such a big deal of it. Find somewhere else to put your things."

It can be a "big deal" if our first concern and commitment is to our own convenience, our own comfort, our own desires and priorities, our own likes and dislikes. This attitude can create tremendous spiritual noise in our hearts. And when a crisis comes into our lives, or we plead for God's help, we may end up crying, "O God, why aren't you answering me?"

SUMMARY

Having our wants too high, especially when they are driven by selfishness, is another serious source of interference in the fine tuning of our lives, and therefore could be one of the reasons we are not getting answers to our prayers. Jesus gave us what is often called the Golden Rule, which directly counters the concept of selfishness: "Therefore all things whatsoever ye would that men should do to you, do ye even so to them: for this is the law and the prophets" (Matthew 7:12). Joseph Smith said, "Let every selfish feeling be not only buried, but annihilated."[61] And a modern prophet, Gordon B. Hinckley, put it this way: "My plea is that if we want joy in our hearts, if we want the Spirit of the Lord in our lives, let us forget ourselves and reach out. Let us put in the background our own personal, selfish interests and reach out in service to others."[62]

CHAPTER 9

REVERENCE AND THE SABBATH DAY—KEYS TO GREATER INNER QUIET

"Irreverence suits the purposes of the adversary by obstructing the delicate channels of revelation in both mind and spirit. . . . Reverence invites revelation."

—BOYD K. PACKER[63]

SPIRITUAL NOISE

We have previously noted that the voice of the Lord is unique in that it is still, small, and it whispers. With that in mind, it follows that some words that have been used to describe the process of spiritual communication are *refined, sensitive,* and *delicate.*

We speak of a crystal goblet as being very *delicate,* meaning that it is easily broken or damaged and must be handled with great care. When we say that something is highly *refined,* it means that impurities, flaws, and other unwanted elements have been removed. Being *sensitive* implies that a person is quick to recognize or respond to even subtle changes or influences.

> *"These delicate, refined spiritual communications are not seen with our eyes nor heard with our ears. And even though it is described as a voice, it is a voice that one feels more than one hears. . . . [We must] learn to trust those delicate, sensitive, spiritual promptings."*
>
> —BOYD K. PACKER[64]

When we talk about having inner quiet so that we can "hear" the still, small voice, all of these words expand our understanding of what is required. Our privileges with the communications of the Spirit can be easily damaged or diminished. The more we remove the impurities, flaws, and unwanted elements from our lives, the more we are in tune with the Spirit of the Lord. This is why we are talking about things that may be overlooked when we ask why God isn't answering our prayers. In some cases, we may even exclaim, "Really? *That* is all that's holding me back?"

Many years ago, President Harold B. Lee was speaking to a group of seminary and institute teachers and asked them this question: "What is the most serious sin that you can commit?" Immediately the teachers fired answers at him: blasphemy against the Holy Ghost, becoming a son of perdition, murder, adultery, and so on. He kept shaking his head. Then, when they had no more guesses, he said something like this: "The most serious sin *you* can commit is the one that keeps *you* out of the celestial kingdom. If we don't achieve the opportunity to return and live with God, does it really make a lot of difference what it was that kept us out?"

What a powerful insight. How grateful we should be if it is not infidelity, or pornography, or some other serious immoral behavior that is keeping us from revelation, for the repentance process in such cases is much more stringent and difficult. But the Lord makes it clear that those who have covenanted to be His disciples are held to a higher standard even in lesser things: "For of him unto whom much is given much is required; and he who sins against the greater light shall receive the greater condemnation" (D&C 82:3).

The Apostle Paul used this analogy: "When I was a child, I spake as a child, I understood as a child, I thought as a child: but when I became a man, *I put away childish things*" (1 Corinthians 13:11). With that higher standard of expectation and accountability, we must look at any and every possible thing that is interfering with our ability to pick up these delicate, sensitive, and refined messages we call revelation, which is how many of our prayers are answered.

IRREVERENCE BLOCKS REVELATION

Latter-day Saints are a gregarious and social people. We like each other, for the most part, and like to be together. Often our wards and branches become like extended families, and close friendships and warm associations are formed. So it is not surprising that sometimes when we get together, it feels a little like a family re-union. And unfortunately, that too often is true on Sundays as well. We greet each other warmly in the halls, and often continue those boisterous conversations as we move into the chapel. Missionaries return home and speak in sacrament meetings; extended family, along with friends and former mission associates, come up after-wards to welcome them home. We gather around them with hugs and back slaps and hearty congratulations, not exactly using our "temple voices."

President Packer once gave a conference talk titled "Reverence Invites Revelation," in which he made a sobering observation: "Our sacrament and other meetings need renewed attention to as-sure that they are truly worship services in which members may be spiritually nourished and have their testimonies replenished and in which investigators may feel the inspiration essential to spiritual conversion. . . . When we step into the chapel, we must!—each of us must—watch ourselves lest we be guilty of intruding when someone is struggling to feel delicate spiritual communications. Leaders sometimes wonder why so many active members get them-selves into such predicaments in life. Could it be that they do not feel what they need to feel because our meetings are less than they might be spiritually?"[65]

Our first reaction to that statement might be, "Really? Being noisy in sacrament meeting could be directly contributing to our inability to deal with life's challenges?" But remember those three words President Packer used in the opening quote to this chapter: "Reverence invites revelation." He doesn't say that being more rev-erent will guarantee that all problems will be removed from our lives; only that being more in tune with revelation can empower us to deal with those challenges more successfully. Who would not like that promise fulfilled in their life?

Reverence comes from the Latin *reverentia*, which means a deep respect or awe, especially for sacred things. A lack of reverence sometimes occurs during sacrament meeting as people text or play games on their electronic devices (and we're not just talking young children here) or whisper openly to each other. We sleep, daydream, write notes, and a myriad of other activities, and then absently pop the emblems of the sacrament into our mouths when the deacons bring them by. Occasionally, we even see class instructors using sacrament meeting as a time to prepare their lessons for that day. Surely such actions, which we do without considering the consequences, dishonor both the Father and the Son and offend the Spirit.

Irreverence doesn't occur only on the Sabbath. Irreverence can occur in many other forms and at other times in our daily lives. Any time we dishonor, ridicule, or neglect the sacred, we are being irreverent. We need to be careful that we don't treat sacred things lightly or brush aside sacred covenants we've made in the temple, including how we wear the temple garment. We may view these as minor things, but, as President Lee suggested, if what seems like a trivial thing is the cause of us moving farther away from God, it is not a trifle at all. Note these reminders from the scriptures:

"Sacrament meeting ought to be a time of spiritual refreshment for our people. . . . They gather to partake of the sacrament and renew their covenants with the Lord. . . . We take upon ourselves His name and agree to keep His commandments and He, in turn, promises that His Spirit will be with us. If we could bring about the consummation of that covenant in the lives of our people with a renewal each week, what a marvelous thing it would be. Let us encourage a spirit of reverence in sacrament meeting. . . . Let us see that all that is done is in harmony with the purpose of that meeting."

—GORDON B. HINCKLEY[66]

- "Ye will teach [your children] to walk in the ways of truth and *soberness*" (Mosiah 4:15).
- "Trifle not with *sacred* things" (D&C 6:12).
- "Perform with *soberness* the work which I have commanded you" (D&C 6:35).
- "Let the *solemnities of eternity* rest upon your minds" (D&C 43:34).
- "Remain steadfast in your minds in *solemnity*" (D&C 84:61).
- "Ye shall declare whatsoever thing ye declare in my name, in *solemnity of heart*" (D&C 100:7).
- "All things [are] done in order and in *solemnity* before him" (D&C 107:84).

President David O. McKay gave this wonderful definition of reverence, which shows that it is much more than just Sabbath day behavior: "Inseparable from the acceptance of the existence of God is an attitude of reverence. The greatest manifestation of spirituality is reverence; indeed, *reverence is spirituality.* Reverence is profound respect mingled with love."[67]

"REMEMBER THE SABBATH DAY"

When Moses gave the Ten Commandments to the children of Israel, the first three defined how we are to relate to God and were stated as "shalt nots": Thou shalt not have other gods before Him, worship graven images, or take His name in vain. The fourth commandment did not use that language but admonished us to "remember the sabbath day, to keep it holy" (Exodus 20:8). Note that we often quote only the latter part of the commandment, which says to *keep* the Sabbath day holy, but the Lord first commanded us to *remember* it. Also note that this commandment preceded the commandment to honor our parents and the five commandments about how we are to treat our fellow man—no murder, no adultery, no stealing, no false witness, and no coveting.

The Ten Commandments are like ten great prototypes of gospel laws. Numerous doctrines, laws, principles, and ordinances stem from each of them. That the Sabbath day should be one of those ten prototypes says much about its significance for us. Yet today, the Sabbath day is widely ignored. Even believing Christians who attend church each Sunday morning often seem to think that satisfies their obligations on the Sabbath day.

In modern revelation, the Lord explains what it means to keep the Sabbath day holy in more detail: "And that thou *mayest more fully keep thyself unspotted from the world* [which is another way of saying be holy], thou shalt go to the house of prayer and offer up thy sacraments upon my holy day; For verily this is a day appointed unto you to rest from your labors, and to pay thy devotions unto the Most High; . . . Remember that on this, the Lord's day, thou shalt offer thine oblations and thy sacraments unto the Most High, confessing thy sins unto thy brethren, and before the Lord. And on this day thou shalt do none other thing, only let thy food be prepared with singleness of heart that thy fasting may be perfect, or, in other words, that thy joy may be full" (D&C 59:9–13). Think what it would do for the flow of revelation in our lives if we truly kept ourselves unspotted from the world.

The Lord said that keeping the Sabbath day holy would be "*a sign between me and you* throughout your generations; that ye may know that I am the Lord *that doth sanctify you*" (Exodus 31:13; see also Ezekiel 20:20). To *sanctify* means to cleanse and purify, to make clean, which is how we are kept unspotted from the world. Being unholy is not the only reason God may not be answering our prayers, but it certainly is a major one.

A New Commitment, A New Promise

In connection with general conference in April 2015, a general training meeting was held in Salt Lake City, which was then shared via the Internet with the entire Church. President Russell M. Nelson, who conducted the meeting, explained how the meeting had come about. He said that the First Presidency was concerned about members of the Church who were "lost, unknown, or less active." The First Presidency and the Twelve met together in council in the temple to see what could be done to build greater faith in the members and help them deepen their testimonies. They decided that the best thing to do was to "focus on the prevention of those kinds of problems." They then decided that the best way to help members strengthen faith and deepen testimony was to emphasize the importance of keeping the Sabbath day holy. President Nelson then said: "The Lord's commandment to hallow the Sabbath day and keep it holy is a charge we take very seriously and literally. If we can really do that, *we will help our members to build faith in the Lord and deepen their conversion* to Him and to His Church."[68]

Elder M. Russell Ballard then explained in more detail how they had come to that conclusion: "Of all of the organizational and policy changes or doctrinal training that could hasten the work of salvation at this time, we [the First Presidency and the Quorum of the Twelve] determined that *elevating the spirit and power of the Sabbath day would be the most influential in drawing members and families closer to the Lord Jesus Christ.* . . . I remind you once more, our primary goal is for everyone to have a spiritual experience and a strengthening faith in our Heavenly Father and the Lord Jesus Christ *through Sabbath day observance.* . . . Surely we can expect that cell phones and iPads, games and food can be set aside for one precious hour out of one hundred sixty-eight hours in a week for the sacrament meeting that is devoted to Heavenly Father and his Son, the Lord Jesus Christ."[69]

This should give us much to ponder. Every year, Church members have the opportunity to sustain fifteen men as prophets, seers, and revelators in every ward conference, stake conference, and general conference. And these prophets, seers, and revelators gathered together in fasting and prayer in the house of the Lord and asked this simple question: "What can we do to strengthen faith and deepen testimony in the hearts of our members?" And the answer that came to them was to focus the members on being more diligent in remembering the Sabbath day to keep it holy.

To put it into the context of this book, our prophets, seers, and revelators are telling us that if we want more spiritual power in our lives, more answers to our prayers, more personal revelation for ourselves and our families, then we need to strive more diligently to keep the Sabbath day holy.

SUMMARY

About 700 years before Christ lived, the prophet Isaiah wrote a remarkable passage on the importance of the Sabbath day. He wrote it in the form of a covenant or contract, using the "if/then" language common to such covenants. Here is how he stated it:

IF . . .

- We turn away from doing what pleases us on the Sabbath,
- And call the Sabbath a delight (meaning it really is a delightful, uplifting experience for us),
- And call it (i.e., make it) the holy day of the Lord,

- And call it honorable (i.e., capable of being honored) and actually do honor Him,
- Not seeking our own way, our own pleasures, or our own words,

THEN . . .

- We shall delight ourselves in the Lord (as opposed to being ashamed of our actions),
- He will cause us to ride upon the high places of the earth (traditionally mountains and temples, places of communion with God),
- He will feed us with the heritage of Jacob (whose name was changed to Israel, and who has now become a God and is exalted; see D&C 132:37).

Isaiah concludes by affirming that this is a sure promise because "the mouth of the Lord hath spoken it" (Isaiah 58:13–14).

CHAPTER 10

THREE REVEALED SOURCES OF INNER NOISE

———✦———

"There is a tendency for people to put themselves in the center of the universe and expect others to conform to their wants and needs and desires. Yet nature does not honor that erroneous assumption. The central role in life belongs to God. Instead of asking him to do our bidding, we should seek to bring ourselves into harmony with his will, and thus continue our progress."

—HOWARD W. HUNTER[70]

"A TABERNACLE OF THE HOLY SPIRIT"

In this section of the book we are looking at two things. First, that the voice of the Lord is uniquely different than all other voices. It is still, small, and whispers, and it comes as thoughts and feelings. And second, that because of this uniqueness, even seemingly trivial things can create "inner noise" and make it more difficult for us to receive answers to our prayers.

As we noted in previous chapters, it can be the "little things" we do each day, the habits that we've formed or patterns we've developed, that create this inner noise in our lives. They don't require confession to a bishop or that we stop partaking of the sacrament. But they can still become blockers of revelation and thus hold us back in our progression toward full discipleship.

Most members of the Church are familiar with the opposition the Church experienced through the early years of our history. Mockery, ridicule, persecution, robbery, pillage, exile, and even murder were all the results of Satan's violent opposition to the Restoration.

But there was another kind of opposition. Satan not only waged war against Joseph Smith and the Church; he also fought a bitter battle against the very concept of revelation. If he could not *stop* revelation, he could certainly sow confusion, deception, and misdirection about it.

Part of the problem was that in its infancy, every member who joined the Church brought with them the concepts and culture of their previous religious—or nonreligious—experience. Today many of our youth are seventh-, eighth-, and ninth-generation Latter-day Saints. The "gospel culture" is deeply embedded within them. But in those first years of the Church, every member was a first-generation Latter-day Saint.

One of the consistent problems Joseph Smith had to face in establishing the Church was that every member of the fledgling Church came with many notions that were not in harmony with the restored gospel, including all kinds of misconceptions about revelation. In many cases, their expectations and behavior were totally out of harmony with the Holy Spirit. When these new members were sent out as missionaries, they often carried these misconceptions with them. And they found all kinds of aberration among the new members. Parley P. Pratt described some of these: "As I went forth among the different branches, some very strange spiritual operations were manifested, which were disgusting, rather than edifying. Some persons would seem to swoon away, and make unseemly gestures, and be drawn or disfigured in their countenances. Others would fall into ecstasies, and be drawn into contortions, cramps, fits, etc. Others would seem to have visions and revelations, which were not edifying, and which were not congenial to the doctrine and spirit of the gospel. In short, a false and lying spirit seemed to be creeping into the Church."[71]

To counter these false teachings and practices, Joseph Smith was instructed by the Lord to start a "school of the prophets," where the leadership of the Church could be taught and grounded in true doctrine and correct practices. This was in late 1832 and early 1833. This was a positive approach designed to teach the members, and especially the Church leaders and missionaries, key aspects of the gospel so that they could discern truth and error for themselves (see D&C 88:118–141). We could say that this was the first "missionary training center" in the Church.

The Lord gave Joseph specific, detailed instructions on how this school was to be set up and run. Some of it was basic procedural instruction, but much of the direction was on what to teach and what was expected of the students. The grand, overall purpose of the school was given by the Lord in these words: "And ye are called to do this by prayer and thanksgiving, as the Spirit shall give utterance in all your doings in the house of the Lord, in the school of the prophets, *that it may become a sanctuary, a tabernacle of the Holy Spirit to your edification*" (D&C 88:137).

What a lovely and profound way to describe the grand purpose of what we do in the kingdom of God. Is not this the goal of all that God does for us here on earth? To show us how each one of us can become tabernacles for the Holy Spirit? If that truly happens, then His Spirit will show us all things that we must do to return to His presence.

Those twenty-four verses of instruction given to Joseph concerning the school of the prophets contain much wise counsel for us—counsel that if followed, would increase the likelihood that we can reduce the inner noise in our lives. However, one verse is of particular interest to our study here because the Lord quite sternly commanded us to cease three specific behaviors that directly inhibit our ability to become a "tabernacle of the Holy Spirit." Those three things are: "Cease to be *idle;* cease to be *unclean;* cease to *find fault* one with another" (D&C 88:124).

A closer examination of these three common human frailties will show why these behaviors have such a toxic influence on the flow of the Spirit. Or, to put it another way, these three things may provide possible answers to our question, "Why isn't God answering my prayers?"

"Cease to Be Idle"

This topic may, at first glance, seem a little contradictory to what we said in a previous chapter about how being too busy can create its own inner noise and perhaps hamper our ability to get answers to our prayers. Isn't idleness the opposite of busyness? Aren't we being idle when we take time to sit quietly and meditate about things of worth?

No, definitely not. While one definition of idleness is "lack of activity," that is not its primary meaning. As we have seen, God's precision of language can be very instructive. And so it is here. *Idle* comes from the Old English word *idel*, which means "empty, void, vain, worthless, useless." The Old English *idelness* is defined as "frivolity, vanity, emptiness, vain existence, indolent."[72]

What the Lord condemns here is not periods of rest and putting aside other activities but the devoting of major blocks of time to things which have no real worth, which produce no lasting benefits for us or others. A video gamer can be vigorously engaged in a game for hours at a time, but what benefit, other than personal entertainment, comes from his labors?

When the Lord said, "Cease to be idle," He made it a direct commandment. He did so in an earlier revelation as well, using language similar to that used in the Ten Commandments: "Thou shalt not be idle; for he that is idle shall not eat the bread nor wear the garments of the laborer" (D&C 42:42). The Book of Mormon helps clarify what that means when it states, "Wherefore, do not spend money for that *which is of no worth,* nor your labor *for that which cannot satisfy*" (2 Nephi 9:51). It seems pretty clear that "satisfy" means in ways other than meeting our own basic needs. We think of the spouses and children who are left alone for hours while the other spouse devotes endless hours to sports, hobbies, browsing social media, or other activities. We think of youth who send thousands of texts each month, often to the neglect of studies, family time, personal growth, and in-person social interaction.

We are not trying to compile a list of bad activities here. None of our examples is a bad thing in and of itself (unless the content is immoral, cruel, or hurtful). The problem is not so much the activity but its dominance in our lives to the detriment of spiritual things. Modern prophets sense this spiritual danger and have warned us about it. President Gordon B. Hinckley put it this way: "You [cannot] afford to idle away your time in long hours watching the frivolous and damaging programming of which much of television is comprised. There are better things for you to do. . . . Blogging. Social media sites. Video games. [There is] nothing wrong with them, but to excess they push out the Spirit."[73]

This lack of balance can occur even in our Church service. This is another place where we can be actively engaged but in ways that do not lead to growth and progress. Elder M. Russell Ballard gave this wise counsel: "Occasionally we find some who become so energetic in their Church service that their lives become unbalanced. They start believing that the programs they administer are more important than the people they serve. They complicate their service with needless frills and embellishments that occupy too much time, cost too much money, and sap too much energy. They refuse to delegate or to allow others to grow in their respective responsibilities. As a result of their focusing too much time and energy on their Church service, eternal family relationships can deteriorate."[74]

"CEASE TO BE UNCLEAN"

In the second admonition, the Lord uses the word "unclean." That word may first make us think of various violations of standards of moral cleanliness or the law of chastity. And surely, that is part of the warning. There is no question that a failure to maintain moral purity, including the use of pornography, creates a deafening inner noise that breaks down the lines of communication between us and God. That being said, here we shall focus on another form of cleanliness that we can easily overlook. In fact, some may be surprised when we connect it in any way to getting answers to our prayers.

A short time after the school of the prophets was instituted, something took place in the school that brought another revelation from the Lord. As was the common custom among men at that time, many chewed or smoked tobacco, and they did so when they attended the school. Brigham Young tells us that Joseph became concerned that he had to teach in a cloud of smoke. Emma also complained about having to clean the room of tobacco juice around the spittoons and pick up the cigar butts. This physical uncleanness bothered Joseph enough that he asked the Lord for a revelation on the use of tobacco. He received the revelation we now call the Word of Wisdom.[75] This was just two months after the Lord had commanded the school of the prophets to "cease to be unclean." Could there be a relationship between those two incidents?

Can physical uncleanness and clutter really affect our privileges with the Spirit? There are two things that suggest the answer is definitely yes. The first is a declaration by the Lord Himself. "Behold, mine house is a house of order, saith the Lord God, and not a house of confusion" (D&C 132:8). Clearly, the word *order* has many meanings here, but is not one of them a lack of temporal clutter, uncleanliness, or filthy conditions?

Recently in a ward council meeting, the sister giving the spiritual thought shared this experience: "On Monday, I was part of the group that helped clean our temple. I was given a cloth and asked to dust the celestial room, including the tables and all the woodwork around the walls. I worked for nearly half an hour. When I finished I could not see even the slightest smudge of dirt on the cloth. When I showed it to the supervisor and said something about not getting much for my efforts, she smiled and said, 'Of course not. This is the house of the Lord.'"

Those with children or grandchildren away at college often hear reports on the cleanliness habits of their children and their roommates. One parent wryly quipped, "When I saw her room, I wasn't sure whether to vacuum or rototill." Another said he considered declaring the room a national disaster area and calling out the National Guard. Sometimes, mission presidents and MTC presidents report similar problems in missionary apartments. Surely the Lord cannot be pleased with such conditions.

Elder Larry R. Lawrence of the Seventy gave a conference talk titled, "What Lack I Yet?" He used the example of the rich young ruler asking Jesus what he needed to do to get eternal life. Elder Lawrence suggested that there is great value for members seeking to improve their lives and to draw closer to the Spirit to ask that question of the Lord. He then gave examples of those who had asked that question of the Lord and the answers that came in response. Interestingly enough, they were not great, sweeping declarations requiring prolonged repentance or counsel with priesthood leaders. The answers included, "Stop complaining," "Honor the Sabbath more faithfully," and, "*Clean your room.*"[76]

"CEASE TO FIND FAULT ONE WITH ANOTHER"

Elder Marvin J. Ashton, a member of the Twelve some years ago, described what he termed a "life-style": "I am acquainted with a wife and mother who is chained securely at the present time to a *life-style* of murmuring and criticism. She is the first to point out faults in her husband or to repeat neighborhood gossip. How damaging is a habit that permits fault-finding, character assassination, and the sharing of malicious rumors! Gossip and caustic comment often create chains of contention. These chains may appear to be very small, but what misery and woe they can cause! . . . Retaliation, fault-finding, deceit, pettiness, hypocrisy, judging, and destroying one another do not belong in the definition of pure religion."[77]

This kind of habitual negativity seems to be what the Lord commanded the attendees at the school of the prophets to cease. Clearly *faultfinding* describes something deeper than simply giving needed correction. *Finding* suggests that it is not just an occasional thing. It is repetitive, habitual behavior, an attitude, a character trait, a lifestyle, as Elder Ashton said. It's not just something that we do; *it's the way we are.* And sadly, too often, faultfinding takes place within the walls of the home.

This is a common failing of the human race, but in our generation the current technology has allowed this character flaw to be greatly magnified and disseminated far more widely than ever before. And the anonymity of the Internet seems to have raised faultfinding to new levels of viciousness, pettiness, and cruelty. President Henry B. Eyring taught: "If we look for human frailty in humans, we will always find it. We live in a world where finding fault in others seems to be the favorite blood sport. It has long been the basis of political campaign strategy. It is the theme of much television programming across the world. It sells newspapers. Whenever we meet anyone, our first, almost unconscious reaction may be to look for imperfections."[79]

> *"Unity cannot be manifest nor exercised by fault finding, back biting, complaining about those in authority over us, substituting our ways for the ways which are given to us by those who are our leaders, finding this excuse and that excuse for not doing what we are asked to do."*
>
> —J. Reuben Clark Jr.[78]

Elder Jeffrey R. Holland also commented on this tendency: "Some things we say can be destructive, even venomous—and that is a chilling indictment for a Latter-day Saint! The voice that bears profound testimony, utters fervent prayer, and sings the hymns of Zion *can be* the same voice that berates and criticizes, embarrasses and demeans, inflicts pain and destroys the spirit of oneself and of others in the process."[80]

Summary

Why isn't God answering my prayers?

Perhaps we can answer that question by citing again the counsel given to the school of the prophets: "Cease to be idle, cease to be unclean, cease to find fault one with another." If we follow those admonitions, the promise is that we too can become our own "tabernacle of the Spirit." Think what effect that would have on our ability to get answers to our prayers.

CHAPTER 11

OVERCOMING FEAR
AND PESSIMISM

---

*"Who among us can say that he or she has not felt fear?
I know of no one who has been entirely spared. . . .
We suffer from the fear of ridicule, the fear of failure,
the fear of loneliness, the fear of ignorance. Some fear
the present, some the future. Some carry a burden
of sin and would give almost anything to unshackle
themselves from that burden, but fear to change
their lives. Let us recognize that fear comes not of
God, but rather . . . from the adversary of truth and
righteousness. Fear is the antithesis of faith."*

—GORDON B. HINCKLEY[81]

"God Is at the Helm"

While serving as a General Authority Seventy, I had an unusual experience that changed my outlook on how to view life and especially the future. In the Church Administration Building in Salt Lake City, there is a small cafeteria reserved for General Authorities and their guests. The unwritten protocol is that there are no assigned seats. Members of the First Presidency or the Quorum of the Twelve mingle freely with members of the Seventy and the Presiding Bishopric.

One day early in 2008, after getting my food, I joined four of my associates in the Seventy who were just beginning to eat their lunch. This was at a table for six. As we ate, the conversation turned to current events, particularly the subject that had dominated the news for weeks by that point. It was being called "The Crash of 2007," which would turn out to be the largest crash in the housing market in U.S. history. The Dow Jones Industrial Average had dropped from a record high of around 14,000 points to just over 8,000. Investors were taking huge losses. People's retirement accounts were being decimated. Ominous warnings about the huge debt the government was accruing came regularly. It seemed as though every day there was news of another major financial institution failing. And there seemed to be no end in sight.

Our conversation that day began with someone sharing news of the latest crisis, and then it turned to questions such as, "How long is this going to continue?" "Which big financial institution is going down next?" "How long before things turn around?" One person at the table said that one of his grandchildren was just graduating from business school and despaired of getting a job. Another said that at a recent family dinner, his granddaughter, a college student, said that she wasn't sure she wanted to get married and bring children into such a chaotic world.

And so it went as we ate our lunch. The mood was gloomy and pessimistic. Then, about twenty minutes into our conversation, a senior member of the Quorum of the Twelve came into the lunchroom. When he saw the empty seat at our table, he asked if he could join us. We welcomed him, of course. There was some brief, light conversation, and then our conversation turned back to the same theme with the same pessimistic tone. Each of us raised other concerns or expressed our worries about what the future held. Our new companion said nothing as he ate.

This went on for a few more minutes, and then someone said something like this: "With the huge debt crisis our nation holds, I'm not even sure our country will survive this."

That brought this Elder's head up. He set down his fork and solemnly looked around the circle. Then, as best I can remember his words, he said, "Brethren, the United States of America is the country where God chose to restore His Church. Without the freedoms and protection our Constitution offers, we would not exist. Without the affluence of our people, and the generous contributions they make to the kingdom because of that affluence, this Church could not continue its global operations. So this nation is not ever going to completely fail, because then God's work would fail. We will have our problems, some of them very serious ones, but no unhallowed hand can stop this work. Cheer up. God is at the helm. Do not fear!"

There was dead silence around the table. I don't know what the others were thinking, but I was embarrassed and chagrined. How had we missed something that should have been so obvious to all of us? How had we so quickly fallen into such a pessimistic and negative mood? It was as if a black cloud had settled over our table and now it was suddenly dispersed. This Apostle hadn't taught us anything we didn't already know, so why hadn't we had that perspective before? Why didn't *I* think to say, "Cheer up. God is at the helm"?

"Fear Not"

Such experiences seem to be more common of late. There are many conditions in the world right now that give us great cause to be concerned. War, terrorism, refugees by the millions being driven from their homes, poverty, crime, sexual license, child abuse, sex trafficking, family instability, political chaos, greed, etc., etc., etc. So it is not surprising that when we get together—while out to dinner with friends, in family gatherings, in Church classes, at the workplace—conversation turns to the future and what these crises mean for us and our children and grandchildren. Nor is it uncommon for these conversations to turn increasingly gloomy and pessimistic.

Some may say that these problems have always been with us and that there have always been those who predict the worst. But those of us who have lived for very long know that the decline of values that hold civilizations together is clearly accelerating and increasing. Paul prophesied that in the last days, "perilous times" would come (2 Timothy 3:1). There is good reason to be deeply concerned for ourselves, for our families, for our nation, for the Church, and for the world. Such expressions of concern are normal and do not displease the Lord.

But if we are not careful, we can quickly let negativity and pessimism and despair settle in on us, and that is *not* pleasing to the Lord, nor to the Holy Spirit. Discouragement, despair, and fear can become a source of inner noise that dampens our ability to feel and respond to the Spirit and could affect our ability to get answers to our prayers.

This is a principle frequently found in the scriptures, and often it comes in the imperative form—not just as a recommendation but as a commandment. For example:

- "Take heed, and be quiet; fear not, neither be faint-hearted" (2 Nephi 17:4).
- "I fear not what man can do; for perfect love casteth out all fear" (Moroni 8:16).
- "Fear not, little flock; do good; let earth and hell combine against you, for if ye are built upon my rock, they cannot prevail" (D&C 6:34).
- "Look unto me in every thought; doubt not, fear not" (D&C 6:36).
- "Fear not, let your hearts be comforted; yea, rejoice evermore, and in everything give thanks" (D&C 98:1).
- "Fear not even unto death; for in this world your joy is not full, but in me your joy is full" (D&C 101:36).
- "Fear not what man can do, for God shall be with you forever and ever" (D&C 122:9).
- "Go thy way and do as I have told you, and fear not thine enemies; for they shall not have power to stop my work" (D&C 136:17).

The frequency of these admonitions should give us a clue about how important this principle is in the Lord's sight. And the context of some of these references, given when the Saints were being driven out of their homes or while Joseph was captive in Liberty Jail, show that we are expected to put away fear even in very difficult circumstances.

Why would the Lord ask that we not fear when fear and

anxiety are a natural reaction to things that threaten our peace and happiness? Fear is not wrong in the way that infidelity or embezzlement or fraud or pornography is wrong, but overcoming fear is clearly an important principle the Lord has directed. Something written by John the Beloved to the Saints in an earlier dispensation gives us one possible clue. In the context of speaking of the love of God, he said: "There is no fear in love; but perfect love casteth out fear: because *fear hath torment*. He that feareth is not made perfect in love" (1 John 4:18).

That is an interesting linkage. If we love God—and that also means that we have faith in His love—then we have no need to fear. As one of our popular hymns says, "If we do what's right we have no need to fear" (*Hymns*, 243).

FAITH AND FEAR

Modern prophets have tied fear directly to the principle of faith. President Thomas S. Monson said: "President Stephen L Richards [of the First Presidency] taught, *'Faith and doubt cannot exist in the same mind at the same time, for one will dispel the other.'* My plea is that we will find faith by experiencing faith in action. The opportunity is ours. Let us grasp it and retain it."[82]

Here is a wonderful lesson in fear and faith as told by President Boyd K. Packer: "In [my many] years as a General Authority, I have never seen the Brethren frightened. I have seen them concerned and determined, but I have never seen them frightened. Early in my days as a General Authority, I heard on the radio as I drove to the office, that a bomb had destroyed the large doors of the Salt Lake Temple. . . . As I hurried to the office, I saw across the street at the temple, the cars, the policemen, and so forth. But I had a meeting to attend, so I did not go over to inspect. Late that evening as I returned along the same street I saw the temporary covering of the doors, and all was quiet. It occurred to me then that in meetings during the day with different combinations of the Brethren, I had not heard the subject mentioned. There were other things to do. There was a ministry to perform. How could our attention be diverted from that?"[83]

SUMMARY

Here is an interesting chain of reasoning based on what we have discussed here:

- The Lord commands us not to fear because if we have faith there is no need to fear.
- Faith replaces fear because faith and fear cannot exist together within us.
- If we are fearful, our faith is weakened to some degree, which causes a loss of the Spirit in our lives.
- That loss of the Spirit could be another reason why we are not getting answers to our prayers.

III

Meeting the Conditions Set by the Lord

CHAPTER 12

"SEEK NOT TO COUNSEL YOUR GOD"

———⁘———

"As God is the God and Father of the spirits of all flesh, it is His right, it is His prerogative to communicate with the human family. God . . . has a right to dictate, has a right to make known His will, has a right to communicate with whom He will and control matters as He sees proper; it belongs to Him by right."

—JOHN TAYLOR[84]

In this section of the book we shall look at some of the conditions the Lord has set for giving and receiving personal revelation. If we understand those conditions, then of course we will get better insight into why the Lord may not be answering our prayers. As noted in the first chapter, revelation is defined as God sharing His mind and His will with His children through the medium of the Holy Ghost. It never goes the other direction; i.e., we never reveal anything to God. Therefore, God gets to decide all of the parameters surrounding this marvelous gift. He decides *when* revelation is given, to *whom* it is given, *how* it is given, and *what* is revealed. If we try to violate or ignore these conditions, it will directly affect how much inspiration and revelation flows into our lives.

Yet too often we naively assume that we have control over this process and do things that diminish our privileges with the Spirit, such as attempting to tell God how to do His work. We don't put it in those terms, of course. It comes out more like, "Father, I need an answer by this Friday." "I think the best way for me would be . . ." "Please don't ask me to do something that is unpleasant or too difficult for me." "It would be nice if I had a couple of options that I could choose between."

The prophet Jacob taught this principle to his people: "Seek not to counsel the Lord, but to take counsel from his hand. For behold, ye yourselves know that he counseleth in wisdom, and in justice, and in great mercy, over all his works" (Jacob 4:10). Sometimes, without thinking, that is exactly what we do. Could this be one possible reason God isn't answering us?

The True Nature of God

In bearing testimony, we often say that we know that God lives. And that is a good thing.

But knowing that God *lives* is not the same as knowing what God is *like*. Two people can have an equally strong testimony that God exists but differ widely in their perception of what God is like in terms of His nature, attributes, motives, purposes, and character.

Here are some examples of questions that illustrate how people misunderstand God's true nature. These questions are really questioning God's motives and/or abilities.

- If God is all powerful, why does He let vast numbers of His children live in poverty?
- If God is all knowing, why can't He warn people when natural disasters are about to occur so they can escape to safety?
- God made our bodies, so why won't He just cure cancer and other diseases?

All of these questions about the nature of God have answers found in the doctrines of the gospel, but our purpose here is not to explore those answers. Our purpose is to show how an understanding (or lack of understanding) of God's nature may contribute to us not getting our prayers answered as we hope.

In the *Lectures on Faith*, Joseph Smith taught that there are three things necessary if we are to have faith in God sufficient to win salvation. The first is to have an idea that God exists. The second is to have "a *correct* idea of his character, perfections, and attributes," and the third is to know that our lives are pleasing to God.[85]

In connection with the second requirement, the Prophet also taught that an important thing to understand about God's nature is that all of His attributes are held in absolute perfection. If this were not so, He would be limited in His ability to carry out His word.[86] Joseph then gave examples of how not knowing God's perfections can directly affect our faith:

- If we don't believe that God is a god of perfect truth, then we may wonder if He's telling us the truth when He answers us. That doubt weakens our faith in Him.
- If He doesn't have all knowledge, then theoretically we could ask Him a question He doesn't know the answer to. That weakens our faith in Him.
- If He doesn't have all power, then it's possible we could ask for something that He cannot do. That weakens our faith in Him.
- If He is not perfectly long-suffering and patient then we will lose any hope of being saved, for we are constantly making mistakes.

The point is not to explore the nature of God, but to show that our perception (or rather, our incorrect perception) of God's nature can influence our ability to call down His blessings in our behalf. With that in mind, let us now look at some common misperceptions about God that have even crept into the thinking of faithful, striving disciples.

"A Grandfather in Heaven"

Many centuries ago Nephi foresaw a grievous but common error of our time as he described the thinking that would exist in our day: "And there shall also be many which shall say: Eat, drink, and be merry; nevertheless, fear God—he will justify in committing a little sin. . . . If it so be that we are guilty, God will beat us with a few stripes, and at last we shall be saved in the kingdom of God" (2 Nephi 28:8).

C. S. Lewis described this attitude using a powerful analogy: "What would really satisfy us would be a God who said of anything we happened to like doing, 'What does it matter so long as they are contented?' We want, in fact, not so much a Father in Heaven as a grandfather in heaven—a senile benevolence who, as they say, 'liked to see young people enjoying themselves' and whose plan for the universe was simply that it might be truly said at the end of each day, 'a good time was had by all.'"[87]

Can we not see how such unrealistic expectations about how God operates could be one very good reason why He isn't answering our prayers? What wise parents grant every wish their children demand of them?

Modern prophets have spoken of other ways that our concept of God's nature could offend the Spirit and directly impact our chances of getting our prayers answered. President Howard W. Hunter taught: "If prayer is only a spasmodic cry at the time of crisis, then it is utterly selfish, and we come to *think of God as a repairman or a service agency* to help us only in our emergencies. We should remember the Most High day and night—always—not only at times when all other assistance has failed and we desperately need help."[88]

President Gordon B. Hinckley cautioned: "The trouble with most of our prayers is that we give them as if we were *picking up the telephone and ordering groceries*—we place our order and hang up."[89]

If we are not careful, we can begin to think of our relationship with God as a quid pro quo association. It is a subtle thing, but if we are not vigilant (and with a lot of subtle help from Satan), our expectations are no longer, "If I am obedient and faithful, God *will* bless me," but "If I am obedient, God is *obligated* to bless me." In a word, we think He *owes* us—that somehow we have put Him in our debt, rather than vice versa.

This is one reason Joseph Smith taught that knowing the true nature of God and His attributes is one of the requirements for faith. In this case, a person's incorrect perception is, "God must answer me, because I am faithful," when God may be saying, "If you were faithful, you would not seek to tell Me how to do what is best for you."

SUMMARY

Though it is part of the human condition, which is egocentric by nature, to feel that things need to be done our way, God holds us to a higher standard than that. When we think about it, isn't it the ultimate hubris, the ultimate arrogance, the ultimate audacity, to assume that we—foolish, finite, erring, selfish, quick-to-sin, prideful human beings, who have limited vision, understanding, and faith—somehow know better than God what we need and how and when to fill those needs? Heavenly Father is infinite and perfect in every aspect of His nature and character. And we think we can tell Him what is best for us?

Here is the Lord's counsel as to how we avoid making this mistake: "Trust in the Lord with all thine heart; and *lean not unto thine own understanding.* In all thy ways acknowledge him, and he shall direct thy paths" (Proverbs 3:5–6). And, "Be thou humble; and the Lord thy God shall lead thee by the hand, and give thee answer to thy prayers" (D&C 112:10).

Elder Neal A. Maxwell made this profound observation. "The submission of one's will is really the only uniquely personal thing we have to place on God's altar. The many other things we 'give,' . . . are actually the things He has already given or loaned to us. However, when you and I finally submit ourselves, by letting our individual wills be swallowed up in God's will, then we are really giving something to Him! It is the only possession which is truly ours to give!"[90]

CHAPTER 13

SLOW TO HEARKEN

———— ✦ ————

"We watch. We wait. We listen for that still, small voice. When it speaks, wise men and women obey. We do not postpone following promptings of the Spirit. . . . Never, never, never postpone following a prompting."

—THOMAS S. MONSON[91]

THE CALL TO ZION

More than seven hundred years before the birth of Christ, the prophet Isaiah saw in prophetic vision a heavenly city he called Zion (see Isaiah 33:20; 52:1). John the Revelator also saw the holy city in vision, but he called it the New Jerusalem (see Revelation 21:2).

When Joseph Smith restored the Church to the earth in 1830, most of those who joined were believing Christians who knew of these biblical prophecies. They must have been electrified when they read in the Book of Mormon that Zion was to be built in America (see Ether 13:2–3; 3 Nephi 20:22). Then, Joseph began receiving revelations that also made reference to Zion (see D&C 6:6; 11:6; 12:6; 14:6; 21:7) and confirmed that fact.

Just six months after the Church was organized, Joseph received two more startling revelations. He was told the general location of the land of Zion (see D&C 28:9) and that Zion would be a gathering place for the faithful before tribulation and desolation came upon the wicked (see D&C 29:7–9).

In June of 1831, at the fourth general conference of the Church, a revelation directed Joseph and other Church leaders to go to western Missouri, where they would be shown the location of the land of Zion. They were told that if they were faithful, the Lord would "hasten" the building up of Zion (D&C 52:43).

By late July, Joseph and most of the others who were called to assemble there had arrived. On their first Sabbath day there, Joseph did two things. He dedicated the land of Zion as a gathering place for the Saints, and he dedicated a site for a temple that would be built in Independence. Shortly thereafter, the leaders disbanded and started back for Kirtland. Those that stayed began purchasing land, building homes, and breaking ground for their farms. Just over a year later, nearly a thousand Latter-day Saints had heeded the call to gather to Zion, and more were coming all the time.

We can easily imagine their excitement and anticipation. They were the first. They were fulfilling prophecies given thousands of years before. They were laying the foundations of the Holy City that would help usher in the Millennium. Yet two years later, those same Saints were fleeing for their lives. Women and children were driven out at bayonet point. Many of them were barefoot and in their nightclothes and left bloody footprints in the snow. Houses were burned, crops destroyed or plundered. Some of their men were killed in skirmishes with the mobs.

How could this be? Their dream of establishing Zion was shattered. They had come to build the Holy City. Now they were refugees and outcasts. Weren't they God's people? Hadn't they sold their farms and uprooted their families in answer to His call? How could He stand by and watch them suffer? Why wasn't He answering their prayers?

"When you listen to the words of God and follow them, you will hear more. When you do not listen or do not follow, you will hear less and less until finally you may not hear at all."

—HENRY B. EYRING[92]

On December 16, 1833, Joseph Smith received a revelation that answered those questions with great specificity. Its opening lines were not what the Saints had hoped to hear: "Verily I say unto you, concerning your brethren who have been afflicted, and persecuted, and cast out from the land of their inheritance—*I, the Lord, have suffered the affliction to come upon them, wherewith they have been afflicted, in consequence of their transgressions; . . . Therefore, they must needs be chastened and tried, even as Abraham, who was commanded to offer up his only son.* For all those who will not endure chastening, but deny me, cannot be sanctified. Behold, I say unto you, *there were jarrings, and contentions, and envyings, and strifes, and lustful and covetous desires among them;* therefore by these things they polluted their inheritances" (D&C 101:1–6).

And then came a stinging rebuke and specific explanation as to why the tragedy had occurred. In it, there is a lesson for all of us today: "They were *slow to hearken unto the voice of the Lord their God;* therefore, the Lord their God is *slow to hearken unto their prayers,* to answer them in the day of their trouble. In the day of their peace they esteemed lightly my counsel; but, in the day of their trouble, of necessity they feel after me" (D&C 101:7–8).

From their mistakes we learn another condition that God sets for the giving and receiving of personal revelation: when revelation is given, we are not only required to hearken to the counsel given but to do it without delay.

LIKENING THE SCRIPTURES

There were a lot of extenuating circumstances that contributed to the expulsion of the Saints from Jackson County. There were vast differences between the local settlers and the incoming Saints, which created natural conflict. But the Lord didn't mention those in the revelation. He pointed to personal failings unbecoming for those who called themselves Saints. When the crisis struck and the violence erupted, surely the Saints were pleading with the Lord to hear their prayers and intervene in their behalf. When that didn't happen, did some of them cry out, "Why isn't God answering us?"

Here is an interesting chain of logic: 1. The early members covenanted to be Saints when they were baptized. 2. They were to go to Missouri and lay the foundations of Zion. 3. Once there, they didn't act like Saints in some ways. There were jarrings, contentions, etc. 4. These attitudes and behaviors resulted in them being slow to hearken to God's word. 5. This led God to be slow in hearkening to their cries when the crisis hit. That is the answer to their question, "Why isn't God answering us?"

Nephi taught that we are to liken the scriptures unto ourselves (see 1 Nephi 19:23), so let's do that here. Though section 101 of the Doctrine and Covenants was given in direct response to what was happening in Missouri in 1833, God obviously knew that this revelation would eventually be read by many generations of Latter-day Saints to come and undoubtedly that it would help us answer our title question, "Why isn't God answering my prayers?"

Some may be asking why the Lord allowed the Saints to suffer such persecution in the first place. Clearly they weren't perfect, but they were certainly living several cuts above the Missourians that formed the mobs and drove them from the county. It appears that the Lord was punishing the righteous while He let the wicked go unpunished. Why?

One thing we learn from another revelation is that members of The Church of Jesus Christ and others who are striving to be disciples of Jesus Christ are held to a higher standard of behavior than those

"Have you ever received and recognized a prompting from the Holy Ghost, and then decided to respond to it later? And then when later arrived, you found that you could not remember the prompting. I have learned that acting upon promptings quickly greatly increases our capacity to receive and recognize the influence of the Holy Ghost. I have also learned that properly recording spiritual thoughts and feelings greatly enhances the likelihood of receiving and recognizing additional promptings from the Holy Ghost."

—David A. Bednar[93]

who are not. We have been given the gospel, the gift of the Holy Ghost, the Church, living prophets, additional scripture, priesthood power, and many other blessings, so we should be expected to do better and to be better. The Lord made that clear when He said: "For of him unto whom much is given much is required; and he who sins against the greater light shall receive the greater condemnation. Ye call upon my name for revelations, and I give them unto you; and inasmuch as ye keep not my sayings, which I give unto you, ye become transgressors; and justice and judgment are the penalty which is affixed unto my law" (D&C 82:3–4). Clearly this standard applies to us receiving answers and help from the Lord in our day just as it did to the early Saints in Missouri.

SUMMARY

Recently, the bishop of a young single adult ward made this observation: "I often have members of my ward—both males and females—come to me, bothered with where they are in their lives. Many of them are returned missionaries. All but a few are active in the Church and faithfully serve in their callings. Some come in with problems they know they need to resolve, but others come because they seem to be 'drifting in life,' as one of them put it. They say things like: 'I don't feel the Spirit like I did on my mission.' 'I've been trying to decide what to do with my life, but nothing seems to be coming.' 'It's like I have lost my direction, and I don't know how to get back on track.' 'I'm just not happy with myself anymore. What am I doing wrong?' And so on.

"After listening to them," the bishop went on, "I begin by asking them some questions. At first it surprised me how similar the answers are. Now I have come to expect it. The dialogue goes something like this:

"Bishop: 'Are you studying your scriptures?'

"Member: 'Uh . . . well, not as much as I should.'

"Bishop: 'And how often is that?'

"Member (with an embarrassed shrug): 'Maybe once a week. Sometimes less.' Others say, 'Maybe once or twice a month.' Some admit, 'I haven't read them for months.'

"Bishop: 'And are you saying your prayers?'

"Member: 'Uh . . . well, not as often as I should.'

"Bishop: 'And how often is that?' And when they respond in the same way, I say, 'Maybe that's your answer.' I ask them about the temple. I ask them if they are truly making the sacramental covenant each week, and other things like that. Then we make a plan and commit them to it. Invariably, if they are diligent, within a week or two they are amazed at the change. 'I've found myself again,' one sister said with tears in her eyes. 'Why didn't I see that before?' said a young man as he thanked me for my help."

Why isn't the Lord answering us? Perhaps it's because we are slow to hearken unto His voice. If that is the case, why are we surprised when His response is, "Therefore, I am slow to hearken unto yours."

CHAPTER 14

WE TAKE NO THOUGHT
BUT TO ASK

———— ✑ ————

"If thou shalt ask, thou shalt receive revelation upon revelation, knowledge upon knowledge, that thou mayest know the mysteries and peaceable things— that which bringeth joy, that which bringeth life eternal."

—DOCTRINE AND COVENANTS 42:61

Meeting the Conditions Set by the Lord

In this chapter we shall examine a principle the Lord taught to Oliver Cowdery. It is closely associated with the principle of spiritual self-reliance but is of special interest to us because this is a case where a faithful, believing person asked the Lord for a particular blessing but did not get the answer he had expected. And, like so many of us, his natural response was, "Why isn't God answering me?"

Here is the setting. Oliver had come to Harmony, Pennsylvania, to serve as scribe for Joseph in the translation of the Book of Mormon. Considering what an incredible experience that was for Joseph, it is not surprising that not long into the process, Oliver asked him if he might have the privilege of translating as well. Joseph put his question to the Lord, and the response was yes (see D&C 8).

We are not told how long Oliver tried his hand at translation or how he went about his attempt. What we do know was that he failed in his efforts. What a bitter disappointment that must have been for him. Surely he must have wondered why he had not been successful, what he had done wrong.

A short time later, Joseph received a revelation specifically for Oliver. In it, Oliver was admonished to be patient and, for the time being, to be content in his role as scribe. But embedded within the revelation (section 9 of the Doctrine and Covenants) was a specific explanation for why Oliver had failed in his attempt. In that explanation, the Lord taught us all an important principle about what not to do when we are seeking answers to our prayers: "Behold, you have not understood; you have supposed that I would give it unto you, *when you took no thought save it was to ask me*" (D&C 9:7). Which of us has not been guilty of that at some point in our lives? We kneel and earnestly pray for God's help or an answer to a question we have. And because we are sincere, we decide that is enough. So we sit back and wait for the answer to come.

After His gentle rebuke, the Lord went on and told Oliver what he should have done in addition to asking: "But, behold, I say unto you, that *you must study it out in your mind;* then *you must ask me if it be right,* and if it is right I will cause that your bosom shall burn within you; therefore, you shall feel that it is right. But if it be not right you shall have no such feelings, but you shall have a stupor of thought that shall cause you to forget the thing which is wrong; therefore, you cannot write that which is sacred save it be given you from me" (D&C 9:8–9).

Note that the word *it* is used five times in that passage. But in context, there is no antecedent to clearly define what "it" means. And to make it more complicated, it appears that "it" could refer to two different things. Let us examine what the Lord says closely.

"You must study it out in your mind." For Oliver, that seems to refer to whatever passage from the Book of Mormon manuscript he was given to translate. For us, "it" seems to refer to whatever issue or question it is that we have brought to the Lord. We are to gather as much information as we can about it. We must consider the possibilities. We must ponder and wrestle with the issue, weighing the pros and cons of how we proceed.

"Then you must ask me if it be right." If what is right? What immediately follows gives us the context for the second "it." In the "studying out" process, we will normally start to have feelings about what makes the most sense or seems to provide the better option. In other words, we start moving toward a conclusion of sorts or we make a tentative decision as to the best answer. And that gives us a context for what the Lord meant when He said, "Ask me if *it* be right." This changes the nature of our prayers. Instead

of saying, "Tell me what I need to do," we now say something like this: "I think that this choice might be the correct decision or the best way to go. Am I right? Is *it* (my conclusion) correct?"

This latter question is acceptable to the Lord, for now we are following the counsel given in D&C 58:26–29. We are not expecting to be told every little thing that we should do. We are choosing things through our own free will.

And when we do this, the Lord promises us one of two answers: "If *it* [our conclusion or decision] is right I will cause that your bosom shall burn within you; therefore, you shall feel that it is right. But if *it* be not right you shall have no such feelings, but you shall have a stupor of thought that shall cause you to forget the thing which is wrong."

The Lord is very clearly teaching us that simply asking Him to solve our problems for us is not sufficient. And if, like Oliver, that is all we do, we shouldn't be surprised when the Lord doesn't answer us.

President Thomas S. Monson made personal application of Oliver's experience to our own situation: "What will be my faith? Whom shall I marry? What will be my life's work? I am so grateful that we need not make those decisions without eternal help. Each one of us can have the guidance and direction of Heavenly Father if he strives for it. I would encourage us to learn and memorize the ninth section of the Doctrine and Covenants. This is a section that is frequently overlooked but that has a lesson for all of us. When we contemplate making a significant decision, may I suggest we go to our Heavenly Father in the manner in which the Prophet Joseph indicated the Lord advised [Oliver Cowdery]. . . . Such is inspired direction for us in our day."[94]

The Burning of the Bosom and the Stupor of Thought

Let us now turn to the Lord's explanation of how He will send confirmation to us about whether the decision is right or wrong. As noted, He used two phrases:

The burning of the bosom. Sometimes, we tend to take scriptural language literally and this leads to misunderstanding. Many have assumed that the burning of the bosom describes an actual, physical heat that we will feel inside of our bodies. The Lord clarified that phrase by adding, "you shall *feel that* it is right" (D&C 9:8). That should remind us of what we discussed in Chapter 4 on the unique nature of the voice of the Lord. In D&C 8:2–3, we are told that the Spirit speaks to our mind and to our heart. In other words, the majority of revelation comes as thoughts and feelings. So the question is, can this burning of the bosom be a literal burning, or does it refer to the feelings we have inside of us? It is possible that for some it might actually come with a sensation of heat. After all, the Lord can manifest His will to us any way He chooses. But modern prophets have suggested that it is most often the latter.

President Boyd K. Packer described it this way: "This burning in the bosom is not purely a physical sensation. It is more like a warm light shining within your being."⁹⁵

The stupor of thought. The Lord says the stupor of thought will cause us to "forget" a wrong choice (D&C 9:9). That seems odd. As one person put it, "How is that possible? I've been troubled by this question for weeks or months, and suddenly I wake up one morning and think, *Now, what was that problem I've been worrying about for so long?*" Of course not. The burning of the bosom was a metaphor for the feeling of positive confirmation. The stupor of thought seems to be a similar expression.

Here is another case in which we benefit from understanding a word's meaning in Joseph Smith's time. To us, *forget* means that we can't remember something. But in the *Online Etymological Dictionary*, it notes that the construction of *for-get* could be rendered as *un-get*. The idea is that the thing isn't necessarily removed from our memory but that its importance to us changes, and we "un-get" the feelings we had before.

What the Lord seems to suggest here is that the idea we once strongly felt will lose its appeal and we will let it go from our mind and look for another option.

Summary

We close this chapter with this counsel from Elder Dieter F. Uchtdorf: "The invitation to trust the Lord does not relieve us from the responsibility to know for ourselves. This is more than an opportunity; it is an obligation—and it is one of the reasons we were sent to this earth. Latter-day Saints are not asked to blindly accept everything they hear. We are encouraged to think and discover truth for ourselves. We are expected to ponder, to search, to evaluate, and thereby to come to a personal knowledge of the truth."[96]

brags about that—but her persistent pleadings did eventually change his mind. The judge specifically says he did not help her because it was the right thing to do or because he felt sorry for the woman. He gave in because of her relentless persistence: "this widow troubleth me." To put it in our modern vernacular, the judge is saying something like this: "This woman is driving me crazy. Every time I turn around, there she is again. She texts me four or five times a day. She calls me over and over. She's posting on Facebook and telling everyone what a cruel and hard-hearted man I am. I've had enough. I'm going to grant her what she wants just to get her off my back."

And that's the story.

Another name that scholars have given this parable is the parable of the importunate woman. The word *importunate* comes from the verb "to importune." This word conveys the opposite meaning of "to faint." To faint means to give up too easily; to importune means "to request with urgency; to press with solicitation; to urge with frequent or increasing application."[98] Though that word is not used in Luke's account, it is used by the Savior in modern-day scripture. After reciting the parable, Jesus counsels the Saints to "importune" (the word is used three times) the civil authorities for redress and justice (see D&C 101:81–92).

But here is what seems to be a perplexing paradox. In the Sermon on the Mount, the Savior taught that we are not to use vain repetitions in our prayers because "your Father knoweth what things ye have need of, *before* ye ask him" (Matthew 6:8). Think about that for a moment. "If God knows everything already," as one person rather crassly put it, "then why do I need to pray at all? Why doesn't He just give me what I need when I need it?"

It is a fair question. The request that we importune God with great persistence cannot be to satisfy some petty whim of the

"We need strength beyond ourselves to keep the commandments in whatever circumstance life brings to us. The combination of trials and their duration are as varied as are the children of our Heavenly Father. No two are alike. But what is being tested is the same, at all times in our lives and for every person: will we do whatsoever the Lord our God will command us?"

—HENRY B. EYRING[99]

Lord. Nor can it be that He wants us to jump through some kind of theological hoops in order to prove our submissiveness to Him. But that is the very crux of the lesson the parable is teaching us. It is not about letting God know how desperately we need His help—oh, no. The lesson of the parable is *what can happen to us if He doesn't immediately answer our fervent prayers and yet we don't "faint," or give up.*

This is one very clear lesson we can draw from the parable. No matter how difficult our challenges or trials, the Lord fully expects us to continue in prayer, even if there seems to be no answer forthcoming. Why? Because we are not trying to change God's heart; *God is trying to change our hearts!* Because our Father knows us intimately and loves us infinitely, there are times when He may be saying to us, "This is an opportunity for you to grow in faith, in trust, in spirituality, and in experience. Because I love you, I will not take away such opportunities from you."

DIVINE TUTORIALS

The process of self-examination and subsequent change is so important to our spiritual growth and spiritual self-reliance that sometimes the Lord deliberately holds back because we would miss a growth opportunity if He answered us right away. Why would He intervene and terminate the process before the lessons are learned, before the desired maturing has occurred? To use a very inadequate analogy, it would be like an Olympic track and field coach lowering the hurdles because so many runners are bashing their knees against them and crashing onto the track. On the contrary, once runners push themselves to clear every hurdle with ease, what does the coach do? He raises the hurdles.

Elder Neal A. Maxwell coined a phrase that captures the essence of the lesson of the parable of the unjust judge: "In no dimension of the divine personality of Jesus Christ do we see His love any more fully expressed than in the *divine tutorials* given especially to His friends—those who believe in and who strive to follow Him, leaders and followers alike, rich and poor alike, men and women alike, for He is 'no respecter of persons.' He would not deny these enriching but stretching divine tutorials to any who follow Him, especially those who have already done much to prove their friendship for Him and are thus ready for further lessons."[100]

Tutorial is an interesting choice of words. Tutoring is distinguished from other kinds of teaching, not so much in what is taught but in *how* it is taught and the nature of the teacher. The standard definition of a tutor is that he or she is a highly qualified, private teacher who teaches a single student or a small group of students. And typically this takes place over a long period of time. The word *tutor* has its etymological roots in the Latin *tutorem*, a "guardian, or watcher."[102]

In God we have the perfect tutor, and though He serves all of His children, each of His tutorials is intensely personal and highly individualized. If we will accept Him, He is in our lives for the

> *"Let us trust the Lord and take the next steps in our individual lives. He has promised us that he will be our tender tutor, measuring what we are ready for."*
>
> —SPENCER W. KIMBALL[101]

long haul, not to work quick fixes or undertake minor adjustments. Elder Maxwell went on to say: "Perhaps these divine tutorials carry such a high priority because the more we are fully developed here, the more chores and opportunities we can be given in the world to come—chores and opportunities that, without growth through tutoring, simply could not be entrusted to us."[103]

Almost everywhere we look in the scriptures or in the history of the Church we find examples of these divine tutorials. Some clearly involve painful adversity. None asked for their divine tutorial. And, in almost every case, we see an incremental development that unfolds slowly, testing personal faith to the limit and allowing growth and the development of spiritual maturity and endurance. Joseph of Egypt, Saul of Tarsus, and Joseph Smith each went through long-term, difficult periods of spiritual tutoring before the Lord's full purposes for them were eventually revealed.

And, of course, we have the ultimate example of this in the Savior, whose life was never His own but who was totally devoted to the work of His Father. He once described His mortal life in these poignant words: "The foxes have holes, and the birds of the air have nests; but the Son of man hath not where to lay his head" (Matthew 8:20).

SUMMARY

We can ask ourselves over and over why the Lord doesn't intervene when we are enduring some heart-wrenching trial in our lives. It is tempting to raise a fist to heaven and cry out: "Why aren't you answering me?" Many times, we may be delaying those answers because of things we are doing or things we should be doing. But there are times when the answer is something else entirely. Elder Maxwell called such times "divine tutorials." Others have referred to them as "trials of our faith," "being tested so we can prove ourselves worthy," or the "inevitable tragedies of life."

Why isn't God answering me?

If we listen carefully, we may hear this simple response: "Because I love you."

IV

Drawing on the Powers of Heaven

CHAPTER 16

DRAWING DOWN THE POWERS OF HEAVEN

"We live in a most difficult dispensation. Challenges, controversies, and complexities swirl around us. These turbulent times were foreseen by the Savior. . . . God so loved the world that He sent His Only Begotten Son to help us. And His Son, Jesus Christ, gave His life for us. All so that we could have access to godly power—power sufficient to deal with the burdens, obstacles, and temptations of our day. . . . When you reach up for the Lord's power in your life with the same intensity that a drowning person has when grasping and gasping for air, power from Jesus Christ will be yours."

—RUSSELL M. NELSON[104]

"Perilous Times"

About two thousand years ago, the Apostle Paul, filled with prophetic vision, said, "Know this also, that in the last days *perilous* times shall come" (2 Timothy 3:1). Those are sobering words, made all the more sober knowing that we are in those last days, and those perilous times are here. In the general conference following the terrorist attacks on the United States on September 11, 2001, President Gordon B. Hinckley described our time with another word, *distress*: "Wonderful as this time is, it is fraught with peril. Evil is all about us. . . . We live in a season when fierce men do terrible and despicable things. I do not know what the future holds. I do not wish to sound negative, but I wish to remind you of the warnings of scripture and the teachings of the prophets. . . . The time will come when the earth will be cleansed and there will be indescribable distress."[105]

Knowing that peril and distress are the givens of our time, finding ways to draw closer to the Lord and to learn how to get answers to our prayers becomes all the more important, all the more relevant. But God knows all things and has given us what we need to prepare for these times and to endure them well.

Now, in this last chapter of the book, we are going to look at a passage of scripture that was given as an answer to the very question we have been asking all through this book: "Why isn't God answering me?" This revelation was given to Joseph Smith in Liberty Jail during one of the darkest moments of his life. Joseph was in despair for his own life and for the well-being of the Latter-day Saints who were, at that very moment, being driven from the state of Missouri under horrendous conditions and with terrible suffering. He summed up his anguish in five words: "O God, where art thou?" (D&C 121:1).

Though God chose not to answer that specific question, what He did give to Joseph that day is an answer of far greater significance, especially to those of us living in the perilous times we see all around us now. And what the Savior gave to the Prophet was the answer to a far more significant and relevant question for our day: "*How do we draw on the powers of heaven to bless our lives and the lives of those we love in these perilous times?*"

To answer that, we shall walk through section 121 of the Doctrine and Covenants, where the revelation is recorded. When we are done, we may find that the ultimate answer to our question, "Why isn't God answering me?" could be, "Because you are not asking the right question."

As we begin our examination of this revelation, I strongly encourage you to open the Doctrine and Covenants and study section 121 as you continue to read.

"How Long Shall Thy Hand Be Stayed?"

When the Prophet Joseph cried out, "O God, where art thou?" (D&C 121:1), he was not crying out for deliverance from his own miseries and deprivations, terrible though they were. He was keenly aware of what was happening to his people, including his own aged mother and father, his wife, and his four children. And there he sat, helpless to do anything other than pray. And when nothing seemed to change, he wondered why God wasn't responding. We can sense the pain and anguish he was experiencing from the questions he put to the Lord:

- Where art Thou hiding? (see D&C 121:1).
- How long shall Thy hand be stayed from helping them? (see D&C 121:2).

143

- How long will this go on without Thine intervention? (see D&C 121:2).
- How long wilt Thou listen to their cries without answering? (see D&C 121:2).
- How long shall they suffer before Thy heart is softened? (see D&C 121:3).

What followed next was not another question, but a direct petition for understanding: "O Lord God Almighty, maker of heaven, earth, and seas, and of all things that in them are, and who controllest and subjectest the devil, and the dark and benighted dominion of Sheol—stretch forth thy hand; let thine eye pierce; let thy pavilion be taken up; let thy hiding place no longer be covered; let thine ear be inclined; let thine heart be softened, and thy bowels moved with compassion toward us. Let thine anger be kindled against our enemies; and, in the fury of thine heart, with thy sword avenge us of our wrongs. Remember thy suffering saints, O our God; and thy servants will rejoice in thy name forever" (verses 4–6).

This change of direction in Joseph's plea is enlightening. The first thing to note is that of all the titles he could have used in addressing God, Joseph referred to Him as the *Lord God Almighty.* That title conveys the reality that God has all power; He is omnipotent. In a word, Joseph acknowledges that God has all power. His question is, why then isn't God extending that power in behalf of His people?

Joseph next pleads for God's intervention, but let us paraphrase his pleas to include this acceptance of God's power and suggest the real questions that were troubling him (see verses 4–6).

- Since God has perfect and infinite power, why isn't He unleashing it in our behalf?

- Our people are not perfect, but considering that our enemies are mobbing, raping, looting, and killing us, why aren't they being punished?
- If God's heart is hardened against us, what will it take for us to have it softened?

When Joseph had finished pouring out his heart to God, the Lord began to speak to him. The Lord's answers are instructive, considering the questions in Joseph's mind.

He tells Joseph to be at peace, that He recognizes this is a terrible time for him and his people, but that it is not going to last forever (see verse 7).

Then the Savior made him a promise: "If thou endure it well, God shall exalt thee on high" and "thou shalt triumph over all thy foes" (verse 8). This is interesting, for Joseph wasn't asking for anything for himself.

In what must have felt like a gentle but loving rebuke, the Lord told Joseph that it could be worse. Job had lost his friends and family, who accused him of being punished for his wickedness. Joseph's friends were standing by him and would soon greet him warmly (see verses 9–10).

As for the Missourians, though it might look as though there were no consequences for their terrible deeds, the Lord described what awaited them for their wickedness. It is one of the most detailed and damning condemnations of the wicked found in all of scripture (see verses 11–25).

And as for Joseph not understanding why God was doing what He was doing, the Lord promised Joseph that the time was coming when God would give him and the Saints all kinds of knowledge and wisdom, even the mysteries of eternity (see verses 26–33).

And Why Are They Not Chosen?

The Lord then asked a question of His own, and answered it: "*What power shall stay the heavens?* As well might man stretch forth his puny arm to stop the Missouri river in its decreed course, or to turn it up stream, as to hinder the Almighty from pouring down knowledge from heaven upon the heads of the Latter-day Saints" (verse 33).

It's almost as if God is saying to Joseph, "You're asking me what powers can stay the heavens? Well, certainly not any power on earth. Let's get that straight." Think of that answer for a moment. Isn't that the question that underpins our title question? When we ask why God is not answering our prayers, aren't we in a way asking what it is that is stopping God from helping us? Is it something we've done? Is it that God doesn't hear us? Is it some other power out there that we don't understand? Here, the Lord makes it clear that it is not due to any limitations on His part.

And then God asks another question of Joseph, and this is the key question for every child of God who has ever or will ever come to earth, though it has specific application to those who claim to be His people: "*Behold, there are many called, but few are chosen. And why are they not chosen?*" (verse 34).

That is the critical question of this whole passage. "*Why are they not chosen?*" Before we examine how the Lord answers His own question, we need to ask two other questions: "*Called* to what? *Chosen* for what?" Only then will the answer to why they are not chosen make sense. Fortunately, a careful reading of what follows next gives us the answers. "Because their hearts are set so much upon the things of this world, and aspire to the honors of men, that they do not learn this one lesson—That the rights of the priesthood are inseparably connected with *the powers of heaven,* and that the *powers of heaven* cannot be controlled nor handled only upon the principles of righteousness" (verses 35–36).

And there is our answer. Many are called to control the powers of heaven, but few are actually chosen to do so. Joseph was wondering why God's perfect power (which could also properly be called "the powers of heaven") was not being extended in this crisis. Now God Himself says that the powers of heaven cannot be "controlled nor handled" except on principles of righteousness.

What follows through the rest of that scriptural passage provides (1) further detail on what people do that makes them lose the ability to control the powers of heaven; (2) some direction on how those powers are to be used properly; and (3) the promises, both for this life and the next, that come when the powers of heaven are used properly. Ultimately, this is a very precise tutorial in why God may not be answering our cries unto Him.

Problems of the Heart

After asking, "Why are they not chosen?" the Lord goes right to foundational causes, and both could be described as a "heart problem." He answers, "Because their hearts are set so much upon the things of this world, and aspire to the honors of men, that they do not learn this one lesson" (D&C 121:35). And there it is. Two things at the core of our spiritual being (for that is what the heart represents in the scriptures) become the root of the problem for us.

To have our hearts set on the things of this world has direct and enormous impact on our ability to call down and handle the powers of heaven. The second heart problem is that we "aspire" to the honors of men. The word comes from the Old French word meaning "to breathe."[106] Since our constant breathing is what maintains life—much more directly than even food or drink—to "aspire for something" carries the connotation of "this is what keeps me alive," or "this is what I live for." It defines our priorities.

The Lord then explains that when either or both of these character flaws define our lives, we don't learn this critical lesson about spiritual progress: "That the rights of the priesthood are inseparably connected with the powers of heaven, and that the powers of heaven cannot be controlled nor handled only upon the principles of righteousness" (verse 36).

SUMMARY

President Russell M. Nelson said this about this journey we call life: "A doctor's ultimate destination is not in the hospital. For a lawyer, it is not in the courtroom. For a jet pilot, it is not in the cockpit of a Boeing 747. Each person's chosen occupation is only a means to an end; it is not an end in itself. The end for which each of you should strive is to be the person that you can become—the person who God wants you to be. . . . Then you will have learned this great lesson: much more important than what you do for a living is what kind of person you become. When you leave this frail existence, what you have become will matter most."[107]

To make it through this mortal journey successfully, particularly in these last days, which are perilous and filled with distress, we need God's help. He offers that help to all by teaching us about the powers of heaven, including what inhibits them and what facilitates them. But the conditions for gaining access to those powers are strict and require a determined commitment to put our lives in harmony with His will.

In Liberty Jail, Joseph Smith was taught what those conditions are. It is a lesson of enormous importance for those of us living in these last days. Why? Because things are only going to get worse, and more and more we are going to be faced with circumstances where we will desperately cry out, "O God, where art thou?" or "Why isn't God answering me?"

President Nelson provides some excellent closing counsel: "I fear . . . that some among us may one day wake up and realize what power in the priesthood really is and face the deep regret that they spent far more time seeking power over others or power at work than learning to exercise fully the power of God. President George Albert Smith taught that 'we are not here to while away the hours of this life and then pass to a sphere of exaltation; but we are here to qualify ourselves day by day for the positions that our Father expects us to fill hereafter.'"[108]

NOTES

CHAPTER 1

1. "Teach the Scriptures," *Teaching Seminary: Preservice Readings* (2004), 74–76.
2. *Teachings of Presidents of the Church: Joseph Smith* (2007), 292.
3. *Teachings*, 160.
4. *The Promised Messiah: The First Coming of Christ* (Salt Lake City: Deseret Book, 1978), 14.
5. *Finding Peace, Happiness, and Joy* (Salt Lake City: Deseret Book, 2014), 38.
6. *On the Path Home* (Salt Lake City: Deseret Book, 2016), 5.

CHAPTER 2

7. *Hymns* (1985), 158.
8. *Gospel Doctrine: Sermons and Writings of President Joseph F. Smith* (Salt Lake City: Deseret Book, 2002), 132; see also Jeffrey R. Holland, "Be Ye Therefore Perfect—Eventually," *Ensign*, November 2017.
9. *Lectures on Faith* (1985), Lecture 3:20.

10. Holland, "Be Ye Therefore Perfect—Eventually."
11. "Morality and Psychoanalysis," in *The Best of C. S. Lewis* (Ada, MI: Baker Book House, 1975), 476.
12. "Healing the Spiritual Wounds of Sexual Abuse," *Ensign,* April 2001.
13. Ibid.
14. "Value beyond Measure," *Ensign,* November 2017.
15. "The Master Healer," *Ensign,* November 2016.
16. *Hope in Our Hearts* (Salt Lake City: Deseret Book, 2009), 61.

CHAPTER 3

17. "Teach the Gospel of Salvation," *Ensign,* January 1973.
18. "Reverence Invites Revelation," *Ensign,* November 1991.
19. "Supporting the Family," *Worldwide Leadership Training Meeting* (February 11, 2006), 5.
20. "Revelation," Address to Teachers of Religion (August 24, 1954), 3–4.
21. In Daniel H. Ludlow, ed., *Latter-day Prophets Speak* (Salt Lake City: Bookcraft, 1951), 292.
22. "The Candle of the Lord," *Ensign,* January 1983.
23. "Revelation in a Changing World," *Ensign,* November 1989.

CHAPTER 4

24. Journal of Wilford Woodruff, January 20, 1872, Archives of The Church of Jesus Christ of Latter-day Saints.
25. "The Candle of the Lord," *Ensign,* January 1983.
26. *Man: His Origin and Destiny* (Salt Lake City: Deseret Book, 1954), 16–17.
27. *To Draw Closer to God: A Collection of Discourses by Henry B. Eyring* (Salt Lake City: Deseret Book, 1997), 29.
28. *Let Not Your Heart Be Troubled* (Salt Lake City: Bookcraft, 1991), 210.
29. *The Lord's Way* (Salt Lake City: Deseret Book, 1991), 23.
30. *Finding Peace in Our Lives* (Salt Lake City: Deseret Book, 1995), 174.

31. *An Invitation to Live the Good Life* (Salt Lake City: Deseret Book, 2002), 62–63.

32. *Teachings of Presidents of the Church: Spencer W. Kimball* (2006), 457.

33. "Line upon Line, Precept upon Precept," Ricks College Devotional (September 11, 2001), 3.

34. *The Holy Temple* (Salt Lake City: Bookcraft, 1980), 107.

CHAPTER 5

35. "The Needs before Us," *Ensign*, November 2017.

36. "As a Child," *Ensign*, May 2006.

37. *Way to Be! 9 Ways to Be Happy and Make Something of Your Life* (New York: Simon and Schuster, 2002), 103.

38. "The Voice of the Spirit," CES Fireside for College-age Young Adults (September 5, 1993), 1–2.

39. "Until We Meet Again," *Ensign*, May 2009.

CHAPTER 6

40. *Teachings of Presidents of the Church: Spencer W. Kimball* (2006), 492.

41. Harold B. Lee, an address given to the Seminary & Institute Faculty, BYU, July 5, 1956.

42. *Random House Dictionary*, s.v. "care," 314.

43. "Of Regrets and Resolutions," *Ensign*, November 2012.

44. "First Things First," *Ensign*, May 2001.

45. "Good, Better, Best," *Ensign*, November 2007.

46. "The Beauty of Holiness," *Ensign*, May 2017.

CHAPTER 7

47. In Jim Bell, *In the Strength of the Lord: The Life and Teachings of James E. Faust* (Salt Lake City: Deseret Book, 1999), 279.

48. *The Lord's Way*, 138.

49. *The Miracle of Forgiveness* (Salt Lake City: Bookcraft, 1969), 145.

50. *Perfection Pending and Other Favorite Discourses* (Salt Lake City: Deseret Book, 1998), 56.

51. In B. H. Roberts, *Defense of the Faith and the Saints,* 1:167.

52. "Beware of Pride," *Ensign,* May 1989.

53. *A Witness and a Warning: A Modern-Day Prophet Testifies of the Book of Mormon* (Salt Lake City: Deseret Book, 1988), 76.

54. "I Will Bring the Light of the Gospel into My Home," *Ensign,* November 2016.

55. *Perfection Pending,* 55–62.

Chapter 8

56. *We're with You: Counsel and Encouragement from Your Brethren* (Salt Lake City: Deseret Book, 2016), 220.

57. "We Are Women of God," *Ensign,* November 1999.

58. "The Candle of the Lord," *Ensign,* January 1983.

59. *On the Path Home,* 151.

60. "Closing Remarks," *Ensign,* November 2004.

61. In B. H. Roberts, *A Comprehensive History of the Church,* 4:230–31.

62. *Faith: The Essence of True Religion* (Salt Lake City: Deseret Book, 1989), 42.

Chapter 9

63. "Reverence Invites Revelation," *Ensign,* November 1991.

64. *That All May Be Edified: Blueprints for Building Spirituality* (Salt Lake City: Deseret Book, 2006), 335; *The Things of the Soul* (Salt Lake City: Bookcraft, 1996), 58.

65. "Reverence Invites Revelation," *Ensign,* November 1991.

66. *Teachings of Presidents of the Church: Gordon B. Hinckley* (2016), 565.

67. *Man May Know for Himself: Teachings of President David O. McKay* (Salt Lake City: Deseret Book, 1967), 26–27.

68. General Conference Training, April 2015. Opening session, segment 2, outline 6.

69. Ibid., segment 12.

CHAPTER 10

70. *That We Might Have Joy* (Salt Lake City: Deseret Book, 1994), 151.

71. *Autobiography of Parley P. Pratt*, ed. Parley P. Pratt Jr. (1938), 48.

72. *Online Etymology Dictionary*, s.v. "idle, idleness."

73. "A Chosen Generation," *Ensign*, May 1992.

74. "O Be Wise," *Ensign*, November 2006.

75. See Doctrine and Covenants 89.

76. "What Lack I Yet?" *Ensign*, November 2015.

77. "Pure Religion," *Ensign*, November 1986.

78. In Conference Report, April 1951.

79. *On the Path Home*, 107.

80. "The Tongue of Angels," *Ensign*, May 2007.

CHAPTER 11

81. *Faith: The Essence of True Religion*, 13.

82. *Be Your Best Self* (Salt Lake City: Deseret Book, 1979), 162.

83. *That All May Be Edified*, 251.

CHAPTER 12

84. In Ludlow, *Latter-day Prophets Speak*, 289.

85. Lecture 3:2–5.

86. See Lecture 5:1.

87. *The Problem of Pain* (London: The Centenary Press, 1940), 31.

88. *Teachings of Presidents of the Church: Howard W. Hunter* (2015), 39.

89. *Teachings of Presidents of the Church: Gordon B. Hinckley*, 469.

90. "Swallowed Up in the Will of the Father," *Ensign*, November 1995.

CHAPTER 13

91. "The Spirit Giveth Life," *Ensign*, May 1985.

92. *To Draw Closer to God*, 38.

93. *We're with You*, 32–33.

Chapter 14

94. *Be Your Best Self,* 134.
95. "Personal Revelation: The Gift, the Test, and the Promise," *Ensign,* November 1994.
96. *We're with You,* 18–19.

Chapter 15

97. "The Challenge to Become," *Ensign,* November 2000.
98. *Webster's Dictionary,* 1828, s.v. "importune."
99. *On the Path Home,* 5.
100. *Even as I Am* (Salt Lake City: Deseret Book, 1982), 46.
101. "Let Us Move Foward and Upward," *Ensign,* May 1979.
102. *Online Etymological Dictionary,* s.v. "tutor."
103. *Even as I Am,* 46.

Chapter 16

104. "Drawing the Power of Jesus Christ into Our Lives," *Ensign,* May 2017.
105. "Living in the Fulness of Times," *Ensign,* November 2001.
106. *Online Etymological Dictionary,* s.v. "aspire."
107. *Hope in Our Hearts,* 168–69.
108. "The Price of Priesthood Power," *Ensign,* May 2016.

INDEX